CHAMPIONSHIP
TENNIS
by the experts

Dedicated to the source of my
meaning, my wife and children.

CHAMPIONSHIP
TENNIS
by the experts

How to play championship tennis...written by the experts—
Vic Braden, Fred Stolle, Chet Murphy, Dennis Van der
Meer, Vandy Christie, and many others.

edited by
Paul Assaiante

Leisure Press
P.O. Box 3
West Point, N.Y. 10996

A publication of Leisure Press.

P.O. Box 3, West Point, N.Y. 10996

Copyright © 1981 by Leisure Press

All rights reserved. Printed in the U.S.A.

ISBN 0-918438-23-3

Library of Congress Catalog Card No. 80-83978

Cover photographs. **Front:** left-courtesy of the University of
California Sports Information Office; upper right-David Madison,
Inc; lower right-Al Murphy; **Back:** Mel DiGiacomo for Avon
Products, Inc. Used by permission of Avon Products, Inc.

Text photographs by Al Murphy except where otherwise noted:
College and Junior Tennis magazine: 10, 16, 18, 20, 25, 32, 38, 41, 68, 74, 82, 90, 97, 104, 115, 125,
    132, 146, 155, 159, 174, 181, 184, 187, 191, and 208.
Dave Shelly, Penn State University Photographic Services: 46 and 100.
Edwin Mahan, Sports Information, University of Pennsylvania: 144
Sports Information Office, USMA: 80 and 95.

With the exception of the articles by Paul Assaiante, Vic Braden, Barry Meadow, David Benjamin,
Fred Stolle, and Dennis Van der Meer, all articles reprinted by permission from the *Athletic Journal.*

Vic Braden's article, "When It's Time to Leave the Club," used by permission of *Tennis Directory*,
ZIFF Davis Publishing Corporation.

Dennis Van der Meer's article, "Tennis Myths," used by permission of the *Tennis Professional*, the
official magazine of The Tennis Registry Foundation and used by permission of *Tennis Directory*,
ZIFF David Publishing Corporation.

Barry Meadow's article, "How to Sharpen Your Touch," David Benjamin's article, "Be Overly
Prepared," and Fred Stolle's article, "A Winning Approach to Tennis," used by permission of *Tennis
USA Magazine.*

CONTENTS

PREFACE

As a sport, tennis has never been more popular. Literally millions of individuals — men and women, boys and girls, young and old alike — are currently enjoying tennis as healthy pleasureable leisure-time activity. The basis for this popularity is that tennis is a game which requires only a minimal financial outlay for equipment, yet returns a maximum degree of "fun" for enthusiasts of all ages.

Championship Tennis by the experts — Volume 13 in the West Point Sports/Fitness Series — is a compilation of articles by some of the most successful players and coaches in the history of tennis: Vic Braden, Dennis Van der Meer, Fred Stolle, Vandy Christie and many more. It is intended to add to the enjoyment of all who are involved with the game of tennis — at any level. The information herein can either provide the reader with a new direction for skill development or reinforce a previously introduced teaching point.

After reading this text, the next step is up to you. Grab a racquet, call your partner, and head for the courts.

ENJOY!

Paul A. Assaiante
West Point, N.Y.
January, 1981

About the Editor:

Paul Assaiante is the Coordinator of Racquet Sports in the Department of Physical Education at the United States Military Academy. Paul directs both tennis and squash instruction, while coaching the varsity teams of both these sports. He is the President of the National Squash Rackets Association and the Secretary—Treasurer of the Eastern Intercollegiate Tennis Association. Paul is a competitive player in both sports and is the author of a monthly column in *Squash News* magazine.

1 THE FOREHAND

THE FOREHAND

By

Paul Assaiante

The forehand is an interesting stroke because it is the stroke that most people pick up easily and utilize most often for their attack. It is also, in my opinion, the stroke which can most easily break down because there are several variables involved in the forehand stroke, and with variables come inconsistency. For instance, throughout the forehand the elbow should be slightly bent and it is this degree of flexion which is difficult to control. Another variable is the fact that the racket is held on the side of the body furthest away from the net. In order to stroke across the body line there must be some torso rotation, and it is the amount of rotation which is also difficult to control. It is because of these factors that I strongly advocate a basic approach to teaching the forehand.

To teach any stroke, we should start with the grip. This is something that will vary from player to player and I feel that the key point to emphasize is comfort. What feels natural and comfortable for a person will usually be what is best for that person. The coach should not attempt to initiate a radical change of the player's grip unless it is clearly counter productive to good mechanics. The goal is to contact the ball with a vertical racket head and if a person has an unusual grip, he will usually alter his stroke in order to achieve this. The best examples of unusual strokes caused by unorthodox grips would be Bjorn Borg and Harold Solomon. They use western grips and as a result have some remarkable racket movements on their forehands. But, I would not teach it that way, nor would I attempt to change theirs. I was taught to use a continental grip for all strokes, but I normally teach a beginner, who will usually have a weak wrist, the Eastern Forehand Grip. This grip places the meat of the hand directly behind the racket which allows a player to hit natural topspin without any wrist roll.

Photos #1-4 show how to execute a forehand groundstroke. The racket preparation should be early, the weight transfer to and through the ball smooth,
and the application of force should occur in a straight line. These guidelines
are essential on all groundstrokes and are generally well-demonstrated in
photos #1-4. I feel that the racket has been brought back a little too far in
photo #1 and the demonstrator has allowed his wrist to be layed back or
cocked in photo #2. This can be a very serious error in the forehand stroke but
the player has made the appropriate adjustment in photo #3 by speeding up
the rackethead to a locked position at contact. Although this is acceptable, a
firm wrist throughout the stroke is better

The Forehand

Preparation, or the lack thereof, is what gives most players difficulty with consistency on the forehand. It is for this reason that I prefer to teach the easiest of preparations or what I call "the flat-back" preparation. I like my players to pivot while cradling the racket with both hands. The racket should be brought straight back, and to a level just lower than the height of the ball. Make absolutely sure that the racket has not been brought back any further than what would be needed to point to the back fence. The free hand is then brought forward so that it points towards the oncoming ball. This will aid the player in timing the ball as well as in maintaining balance.

The player should then take the steps needed to reach the ball under control. Make sure that the last step is taken with the foot opposite the racket hand (with the left foot for a right handed player, and with the right foot for a left handed player). This last step should be directed at approximately a 45° angle to the net. Stepping directly towards the net will cause an open stance, while stepping directly towards the side line will cause a closed stance, neither of which is desireable.

The player should attempt to contact the ball in line with the front foot. To do this, weight must be transferred forward onto a slightly flexed front leg. The weight transfer will relate directly to the amount of power that the player will be directing through the ball. The wrist must be firm throughout this motion in order to maintain a longer racket-ball contact phase. The longer the phase the better the control. I like to see my players catch the racket with their free hand on the follow through since this tends to lengthen the racket-ball contact phase.

I feel that the racket should have moved in a straight line throughout the stroke. It should have started at a point lower than the height of the ball, and should have finished at a point higher than the point of contact.

The speed of the oncoming ball and the depth that it achieves in the court should determine for the player the length of preparation. A medium paced ball will allow for a full preparation, while a heavily paced ball will dictate a much shorter preparation. On the return of serve, for instance, where the ball has a great deal of pace, an extremely short preparation should be used in an attempt to "block" the ball over the net.

Many of my players seem to have difficulty playing a softly hit, high bouncing ball. This is not an unusual problem because this type of ball will tempt even a high caliber player to take a good whack at it. This ball should ideally be driven back to the opponent high and deep, because there is really nothing that can be done offensively with it.

The forehand must be grooved so that all of its mechanics occur naturally. Many hours must be directed towards this end before a player should be permitted to play games or even points.

FIXING A FAULTY FOREHAND

By

Jim Brown
McNeese State University

In order to reach a level in tennis where you can correct your own mistakes, you must be aware of two things. The first is how a shot should be hit and the second is how you are actually hitting the ball.

There is more than one way to produce a stroke, but there also are some rather specific guidelines to follow. The closer you follow the guidelines, the less chance there is for error. The pros can rely on great athletic ability to overcome unorthodox strokes, but average players cannot. While every shot cannot be executed perfectly, awareness of what you should be doing makes it possible to come closer to the ideal.

That awareness combined with realizing exactly what you are doing with a stroke then allows you to diagnose your problems and to correct them. The purpose of the first in this series of articles is to point out some common problems with the forehand and to suggest some corrective measures.

The first principle of hitting ground strokes is to move. Efficient court movement is apparently difficult for many players because a frequent problem with the forehand is poor position. Poor position means not getting to the ball in time, being off balance when the ball is hit, not getting your weight into the shot or not being able to recover for the next shot.

It is not enough to tell yourself to move. You also have to know when to move, where to move and how to move. The time to move is when the ball leaves your racket on the previous shot. Do not wait to see where the ball is going. As soon as you hit one shot, start moving to cover the open part of your court or to return to the middle of the baseline.

The time to relax is while you are hitting, not between shots. The harder you work to get into position before you hit, the easier the work will be when you hit. Stay on your toes and bounce before you move to the ball, take

15

short steps for short distances and longer steps for longer distances and keep your body low, like a sprinter, as you begin to move.

Understanding how to move may be easy, but moving on the court is more difficult. Here are some ways to help you help yourself get to the ball:

1) In practice, count the number of steps you take between shots. If you are trying to get away with a ready, pivot, swing routine, you are probably having trouble. If you can be aware of taking five to 10 quarter, half and full steps between shots, the increased awareness of your feet moving should help you get to the ball in time.

2) Bounce. Bounce on your toes just before your opponent hits the ball, especially on the serve. Beginners make bouncing look like an unnatural act, but good players make bouncing look as natural as running. Again, the awareness of moving, even if up and down, should help you move toward the ball wherever it goes.

3) Watch your opponent's racket face and try to lean or move in the direction it points as the ball leaves the racket. If you can concentrate enough to follow the ball that closely, perhaps your feet will follow your mind more quickly than before.

Note the excellent use of the free hand for balance.

The Forehand

The second problem may be the backswing—it can be either too late, too big or both. If it is too late, try a practice session in which your partner hits only to your forehand. As soon as you hit one shot, immediately put the racket back for the next. Try to get it back before your shot clears the net. Do that 100 times consecutively if you can stand it. By exaggerating the early backswing in practice, the mind and body may train themselves to avoid a potential problem in a match. You cannot immediately begin a backswing following a shot in a match because you do not know where the next shot will be. But the "early back" practice should leave its mark on your stroke.

If your swing is too big, you will know it because you keep hitting balls late and pushing them off to your right (if you are righthanded). Here are three ways to cure it:

1) Find a hard, fast court to practice on for a couple of weeks. If you can trust your body to find a way to do things right, a fast court should cure an excessive backswing. You cannot get away with a big windup if the ball skids and stays low on a fast court.

2) Practice your forehand against a friend who lines up exactly opposite your position across the net. As you prepare to hit, try not to let the other player see your racket behind the left side of your body on the backswing. Every time your opponent sees your racket, he or she should let you know.

3) Line up with your non-racket side as close to a fence as possible. Have a friend throw or hit balls to your forehand. If you take a big backswing, your racket will hit the fence. A couple of hundred bumps should make you want to shorten your swing a bit.

The real villain in the forehand is the floppy wrist. Lack of strength, poor concentration and just plain poor technique can cause your wrist to move during the stroke. The more movement, the more chance there is for an error. Not only can it move unnecessarily, it can move in several directions. Put your hand out to your side as if your arm is the racket. Now move only the wrist forward in a slapping motion. Many players do that and their shots are sprayed all over the place. Their lucky shots go for winners, but the odds are high against all of that movement being timed just right.

Now, still with your arm and hand at your side, turn your palm up. When some players swing, they let their wrists and rackets slide under the ball just before contact or as the ball hits the racket. The result is chronic backspin, lack of pace and balls that tend to sail. There is a time for shots with back-spin, but that time is not all of the time.

Once more, with your arm and forehand to your side, rotate the top part of your hand forward and down. Wristy players often try to hit topspin by rotating their wrists. If you can do that, you are either very good or very lucky. If you want topspin, keep your wrist firm, start the racket low and finish high. That is easier than hoping your wrist reaches the correct angle at the right time to brush up behind the ball.

Note the tremendous concentration on the ball exhibited by Zina Garrison.

The Forehand

If your wrist is a problem, what can you do about it?

1) Take practice swings with your forehand while locking your wrist into place with the opposite hand. Your motion will be restricted somewhat, but your swing will remain basically intact and your wrist should stay where it belongs. If it moves, you can feel it. Don't let it move. After practice swings, hit a few forehands with your wrist locked in place. When you have a mental picture of how the wrist should look and feel during the stroke, remove the helping hand and hit the ball with a firm wrist. If it moves, start over with the locked-wrist motion.

2) If holding your wrist does not work, use your opened hand as a racket and have someone throw or hit balls to your forehand. By using your arm as a racket, the movement is less likely to take place at the wrist than it is at the elbow or shoulder. Watch your arm move and try to be conscious of the wrist not moving. Again, capture that picture in your mind and try it with your racket. Remember that your racket is an extension of your lower arm. Once it begins to move forward, the whole thing—arm, wrist, hand and racket—moves together as one unit.

3) If your wrist turns with the impact of the ball, you may need to increase strength in those muscles that can keep the wrist steady. There are no gimmicks to help you here. Strength can be increased by playing more tennis or lifting weights. Take a three- or five-pound dumbell, extend your arm out to your side and alternately raise and lower the weight. Begin with five repetitions daily and try to gradually increase the number of repetitions or the amount of the weight.

The last thing that can go wrong is the follow-through. Failure to complete and hold the follow-through momentarily results in a punching motion and a shot without pace or depth. Follow through out in the direction you want to place the ball, across the front of your body and upward, in that order. Carry the ball on the strings as long as you can.

If a poor follow-through is the problem, think about posing for a photograph at the end of your stroke. How would you look if someone took your picture after every forehand? Try it in practice. Hit your shot, hold your follow-though long enough for the photo, then return to the ready position.

Thinking about making your entire stroke look good enough for a picture might be used as a corrective technique to solve any forehand problem. If you know how you should look, take a mental photograph of yourself during the stroke. But do not let preoccupation with form interfere with winning tennis matches. Use your mental pictures as a checklist before you play and correct your flaws in practice.

2 THE BACKHAND

THE BACKHAND

By

Paul Assaiante

Most people develop a game style which is based upon attacking their opponent's backhand. The knowledge of this should serve as a word to the wise for all players to develop their own backhand, in an attempt to at least neutralize this pressure. Several years ago, when I was attempting to develop my own game, I read that many professionals declared they had better backhands than forehands. This concept challenged my imagination and so I set out to learn as much as I could about this stroke. The evidence that I was able to unearth definitely led me to believe that several factors enable the backhand to be a more efficient and effortless stroke than the forehand.

Remember, in my article on the forehand, I mentioned that one variable was a flexed elbow. In the backhand, we do not have this problem because we stroke with a straight arm. I have also previously mentioned in this book that to hit a forehand you must stroke across the body line and in so doing, must initiate some torso rotation. On the backhand, however, we do not have this problem because we are hitting the ball with the stroking side of the body closest to the net. This allows the arm to move forward easily without any body twisting.

If there is one inherent problem with the backhand, it would be racket stability caused by the grip used. I was taught to use a continental grip for all shots, and I prefer that my players use a similar grip for their own backhand. The problem with all of the backhand grips that I have ever seen, however, (except for the two-handed backhand which I will not cover in this article) is that there is very little placed behind the racket handle. With the continental grip, all you have to use for leverage is your thumb and a small portion of your hand. On the forehand stroke, you have the entire hand and forearm behind the racket grip at contact. The result is that you can badly mistime your forehand yet still salvage the stroke, but your timing on the backhand must be much more acute. I teach my players that, because of this grip inadequacy, they must rely on racket head speed rather than on strength to hit an efficient backhand.

I feel that the proper ready position is instrumental for a good backhand. The person should cradle the racket with the free hand while it is held at approximately waist height with the racket head slightly higher. The feet should be shoulder-width apart, knees slightly flexed, and with the weight of the body over the balls of the feet.

As soon as you are certain that the ball is coming to your backhand side, you should pivot so that the racket leads in your preparation. It should be kept at the same height in relation to your body and should never rise above your shoulder during the preparation phase. The wrist must be firm and, as in the ready position, the elbow will still be slightly flexed. It is very important that the free hand still has a good grasp upon the throat of the racket.

You should then take whatever steps are necessary to reach the ball under control. The last step should be with your front foot and it should be taken at a 45° angle to the net. This angle will allow the racket to move forward naturally without being impeded by any torso rotation.

At this point the racket arm will straighten out, the free hand will release the racket, and you should have your weight on the front foot. This will give you a feeling of coiled readiness as you prepare to unleash into the ball. Throughout the stroking phase of the backhand, you arm should be straight and your wrist must be firm. The racket should move in a straight line which would have started at a point lower than the height of the ball, and would have finished higher than the point of contact. This will give you a feeling of lifting the ball over the net, and will give the ball natural topspin. For all of these things to be effective, you must strike the ball out in front of your lead foot.

There tends to be a much greater variety of spins utilized on the backhand than on the forehand, and since there is some merit to each of them, a brief discussion is in order.

Underspin is accomplished by moving the racket from high to low in relation to the ball. It is most effectively utilized when playing high bouncing balls, when returning very wide balls, when returning serve, or at any time that you are placed on the defensive. An underspin approach shot is also a very effective shot since the ball will tend to skid and be much more difficult for your opponent to hit as a passing shot. The sliced backhand as well as the topspin backhand tend to go more naturally cross court. It is wise not to try to fight this tendency because it will often cause an error.

The flat backhand will be hit when the racket moves parallel to the ground throughout the stroke. It will have a good deal of pace and very little spin which tends to make it a dangerous, low percentage shot. The flat backhand goes naturally down the line.

The Backhand

Photos #1-6 depict the backhand groundstroke. The racket is brought back early and really should be a little closer to the body. In photo #4, the player steps into the ball in order to achieve a feeling of coiled readiness. At this point, the racket is released with his free hand and his arms are spread naturally in order to maintain balance. Note that his arm is straight throughout the stroke and that his weight is transferred to and through the ball in a smooth motion. A "jerky" stroke results in a loss of control. Photos #7, 8, and 9 simply demonstrate the three key phases of the backhand stroke: the full preparation phase, the contact point, and the follow-through phase.

1   2   3

4   5   6

7   **8**   **9**

Underspin ground strokes tend to take a good deal of pace off the ball and are widely used during clay court tennis. Topspin ground strokes can be attacked much more aggressively and make much better passing shots.

I have found that as long as your preparation is early, you will rarely get handcuffed by an oncoming ball. Even balls hit deep to your backhand side can be easily taken on the rise in the same manner as you would execute a half volley. Remember that a chain is as strong as its weakest link, and that your game can only be as strong as your weakest stroke. If it is your backhand, then I recommend that you go to a basic flat-back preparation, straighten your arm, firm up your wrist and practice.

Note the straight arm and firm wrist at contact.

ARE YOU LATE ON THE BACKHAND?

By

Vince Eldred
Tennis Professional

Being consistently late on the backhand ground stroke is a common mistake among beginning tennis players as well as those who are not new to the game. Why? Too many attempt to have the foot and the racket arrive at the contact point, racket meeting ball, simultaneously.

The correct procedure is to analyze the shot, stroke an imaginary ball and take a practice swing. Notice what part of the body starts the shot. The answer should be the right foot.

As the right foot starts to move diagonally forward, the player's body weight shifts from his left to right foot. The racket, without appreciable pause, comes right behind the right foot. However, the right foot starts the shot (backhand). If it is executed correctly, the swing is almost an aftermath.

Try the following to solve the timing problem. As the approaching ball bounces, the player should think that he must step with his right foot, diagonally and forward, which presses a button making the ball pop up to him. The split-second delay between the pressing of the button and hitting the backhand is what is meant by the swing is almost an aftermath. By simply considering the right foot presses a button removes from the player's mind all thoughts and worries about the real problem—timing. His only concern when using this system is to press the button with his right foot, and the ball will come up to him at the desired spot. With a little concentration, this will work with any backhand stroke, by simply pressing the button.

Photo "Series A" shows the incorrect way to hit the backhand stroke. The proper way to stroke the backhand is demonstrated in "Series B".

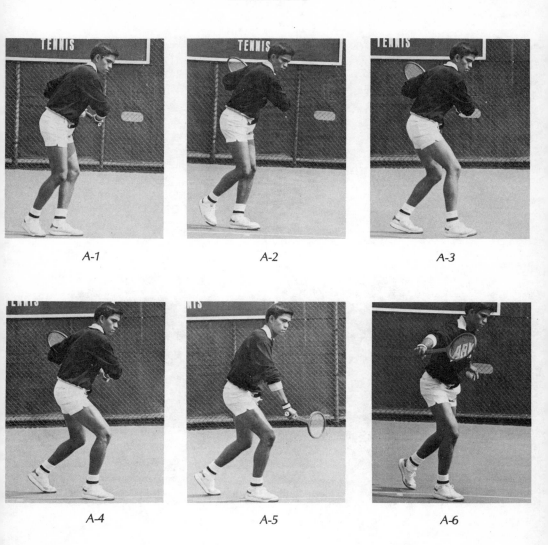

A-1   A-2   A-3

A-4   A-5   A-6

Series A shows the wrong way to hit the backhand. The player is attempting to step swing simultaneously, instead of having his foot start the shot. As a result, the timing is poor. The body weight has shifted to the front foot too soon, and the racket head lags. Contact is made behind the front foot instead of even with or slightly in front.

B-1   B-2   B-3

B-4   B-5

The correct way to stroke the backhand is shown in Series B. Instead of step-ping and swinging simultaneously, the front foot has started the shot, as it should. There is no appreciable pause between the player's foot and the racket, but the foot does start the shot with the racket head coming right behind.

FAST RESULTS IN TEACHING THE BACKHAND GROUND STROKES

By

Larry Castle
Middle Tennessee State University

There seems to be a strange paradox regarding the backhand. Players who are starting to play tennis and intermediate players feel it is the most difficult of the two ground strokes. Most tournament players feel more confident of the backhand stroke and rely on it during a match. The naturalness that tournament players feel in using the backhand side was not always present. It had to be learned, and proficiency came through hours of practice and repetition.

The instructions offered in this article have been compiled over the last nine years of instructing beginning tennis players in the execution of the backhand ground stroke. There are several minor variations in style and common technique. We found, however, that the following steps produce good results for most students and give them a start on their way to becoming sound intermediate players.

As shown in Illustration 1, the player is in the ready position. He is holding the racket firmly in his left hand, and his right hand cradles the throat of the racket. His weight is on the balls of his feet and his knees are bent slightly. The head of the racket should point toward the right net post. Players should strive to maintain concentration and eye contact with the ball. This fact is important and cannot be overemphasized.

Once the player has determined that the ball is coming to the backhand side (Illustration 2), he must change from the waiting grip (Eastern forehand) to the grip we use for the backhand. His right hand should turn the racket about one-quarter of a turn counterclockwise. The first and second fingers

Illustration #1

Illustration #2

Illustration #3

Illustration #4

Illustration #5

Illustration #6

of the left hand are spread a bit. The player's thumb may either be wrapped around the handle or placed diagonally across the back of the handle. Either is correct and is simply a matter of which is most comfortable for the individual. The change of grips must be practiced and must be made simultaneously with the turn and backswing.

Illustration 3 shows the turn and backswing, which is probably the most important phase in preparing to hit the backhand ground stroke. With the eyes still fixed on the ball the right hand pulls the racket back, the player pivots on his right foot, drops his left shoulder, and rotates his hips so that the left leg is pulled across the body and the left shoulder faces the net.

Preparation for actual contact with the ball is now complete (Illustration 4).

As the forward swing starts (Illustration 4), the player's right hand is removed from the racket. His weight shifts from the back foot to the front foot with the swing. The racket is held firmly and his wrist is as firm as possible. The ball should be met about waist high and hit off the front knee. Again, let us point out that we are working with students who are just learning to play. Our only objective at this point is to see that they meet the ball squarely and get it back over the net.

At contact (Illustration 5), the player's eyes look only at the ball. A firm wrist and tight grip will insure a solid hit. If a ball is hit to the player and bounces low, we simply have him bend his knees to hit the same type of stroke as if the ball were coming in waist high. The same holds true in the case of a high ball. The player simply moves back to accomodate the bounce.

A nice high follow-through (Illustration 6) allows the ball to stay on the racket strings a little longer and gives the player better control of the flight of the ball.

As soon as the follow-through is completed, the player should continue on back to the ready position.

Many things will determine the rate of improvement of the individual player. Good footwork is vital in the execution of any stroke and must be practiced many hours. Natural athletic ability has a great deal to do with the rate of improvement. Attitude and willingness to learn as well as student-teacher rapport are vital and cannot really be measured. Taking all these things into consideration, we concluded over the years that the backhand ground stroke can be learned and need not be a stumbling block in learning to play tennis.

3 THE SERVE

THE SERVE

By

Paul Assaiante

I feel that as a teaching professional, I certainly should do more than just help a student develop strokes. I must teach my pupil certain concepts which will explain to him why each stroke should be executed in a certain way. It is the understanding of these critical concepts that will enable the player to make the proper adjustments whenever his game is just a little off.

On the serve, the primary concept to remember is that the net is an obstacle over which the ball must be hit. Unless you are over seven feet tall, it is physically impossible to hit down on the ball and still get it over the net. Therefore, the ball must actually move up and out from your racket on contact. This statement probably will cause you to ask, What prevents the ball from flying all the way to the back fence? The two factors that help keep the ball in the court are gravity and the spin that you place on the ball. On ground strokes, we help gravity by utilizing topspin. This is accomplished by moving the racket from low to high in relation to the ball. We cannot do this in a pure sense of the serve, however, because on the serve we are contacting the ball with a straight arm and this vertical motion does not allow for a great deal of horizontal motion. We can, however, hit the ball in such a way as to give it both a small amount of topspin and sidespin.

Picture the ball as the face of a clock with all of the hour markings on it. Striking the ball at 12:00 o'clock would give the ball pure topspin, while striking it at either 3:00 or 9:00 o'clock (depending upon whether you are a left or right handed player) would give the ball pure sidespin. Neither of these are possible or practical, but by striking the ball at 2:00 or 10:00 o'clock we can gain a happy medium. The slicing action caused at impact between the racket and the ball would cause the ball to "hook" slightly as well as to dip, as if it were a topspin groundstroke. Remember that the ball has to travel a long distance from your racket to the court and for this reason the greatest force being place upon the ball is a forward one. This will occur naturally as a result of your service motion while the lesser "hooking" and "dipping" actions of the ball will occur as a result of the slicing action between the racket and ball. It is crucial that the wrist snap occur in a straight line so that the strings brush against the ball in a firm manner. This motion would resemble an ax moving through the air as opposed to a motion which would rotate the racket around the ball in a manner which would resemble the action of a lacrosse players cradling the ball with his stick.

Now that this concept has been at least partially covered, let us now move to analyze the service motion itself. As I have said before, I teach my players to use the continental grip when serving because it aids in the generation of spin without incorporating any wrist rotation. The serving stance is important in maintaining good balance as well as in helping you address the shot properly. If I am serving for singles play, I stand fairly close to the center mark on the baseline with my feet parallel and comfortably apart. I would position myself in such a way that if I were to draw a line from my rear foot, to my front foot, to the proper service box, it would be straight. It is important that your weight be evenly distributed between your feet at this time even though it will be shifted forward as you stike the ball.

Your first action during the serve is to bring the racket behind your back in a cocked hitting position. Do not be overly concerned with the manner in which you do this as it will vary from player to player. Just get the racket to the cocked position in the simplest way possible. Elevate your arm high behind you so that the racket is in the "scratch your back" position. This prevents your elbow from pointing downward which would inhibit your rhythm and make it difficult to impart spin upon the ball.

The second action, which really occurs in coordination with the first action, is the toss. Your goals on the toss should be to "lift" the ball from your finger tips with no spin and always to the same height relative to your body. You must toss the ball so that you can strike it while being under balance as opposed to throwing the ball and chasing it. This chasing of your toss causes a great deal of inconsistency. I think about tossing the ball approximately one foot higher than I can reach with my racket and attempt to hit the ball as it has begun to drop from this peak.

The last stage of the serve is fairly easy to accomplish as long as you remember that it greatly resembles the action of throwing a ball. This smooth forward swing should be done while you are on balance, and I feel that at least in the beginning you should practice serving without moving your feet at all. I often teach my players to serve successfully from a sitting position. This is not as difficult to do as you would think, and it gives you tremendous confidence in your ability to serve from a standing position.

Hopefully you will have noticed that up to now I have not even mentioned power or speed and its relation to the serve. The reason for this, in my opinion, is that this is the last of the three priorities of serving. One should be

1

Photos #1-13 demonstrate the correct techniques for serving. Photo #1 shows the brushing of the ball caused by the angular contact between the ball and the racket. Hitting up and out on the ball will create a combination of topspin and sidespin. This combination will improve your service percentage and make it more difficult to return. Photos 2, 3, and 4 show how to execute the modified serve, which is the safest way for a novice to learn a basic serve. Photos #5-13 show one way to execute the entire serve. I use a large loop in bringing my racket up to the "back scratch position". Although this is the way I was taught, let me emphasize that this method is only one (of several) way to get to the power position. Don't be overly concerned with this phase of the motion. Also notice that as I shift my weight forward to and through the ball, I step through with my left foot. Again, let me point out that this is not the only way. Many successful players land on the same foot forward. . . Arthur Ashe and Bjorn Borg to mention a few.

   All good serves, however, have several commonalities:
   (a) The motion should start and finish on balance.
   (b) The motion should be simple but efficient.
   (c) The motion should be continuous and void of "hitches."
   (d) Contact should occur at full extension of the body and racket.
So, keep it simple and enjoy the results!

The Serve

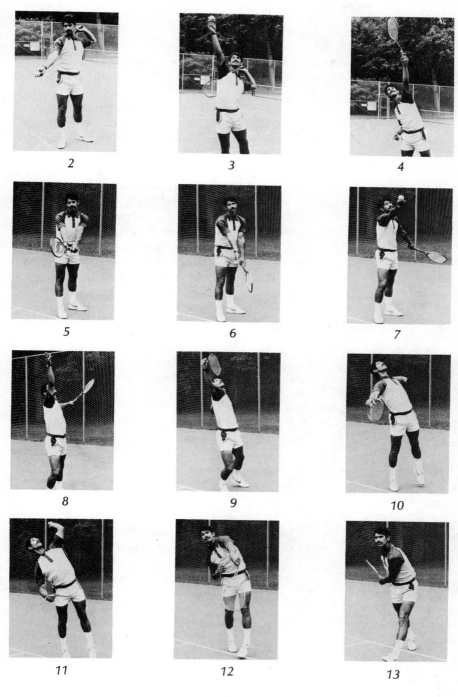

2

3

4

5

6

7

8

9

10

11

12

13

concerned with placement first, spin second, and pace third. Interestingly, most club level players seem to feel that the reverse is true. These are the people who usually hit a cannonball first serve into the base of the net, and a "patty cake" second serve. Most professionals actually hit their second serve as hard as they do their first serve, but most of the force is converted into spin.

I feel that the modified serve is useful in teaching the serve to beginners. The modified serve starts with the racket already in the "back scratch" position. This enables the beginner to concentrate on just the last two phases of the serve.

The beauty of the serve is that you can take a bucket of old balls to the court and practice your serve without the use of a partner. Serve all of the balls, making adjustments for your errors, collect the balls and start again.

At West Point I like to try to end every practice by having the players hit twenty-five serves into each of four service targets. The targets are situated in the far corners of both service boxes. I usually have the players hit 15 second serves and then 10 first serves into each box so that they gain more confidence in their second serve. It will be confidence in their second serve that will allow the players to attack the first serve with more gusto.

Note how the head of the racket stays up long after the ball is on its way.

SERVE FLAT OR SPIN — GET IT IN

By

Vince Eldred
Tennis Professional

In tennis, the server is in complete control of the game. Nothing happens until the server elects to put the ball into play. It is the server's choice as to whether the ball will be served to the opponent's forehand, backhand, or directly at him. The server determines the speed and the type—flat or spin—of the serve. This is the only opportunity in tennis for a player to be the complete master of the situation, so the most should be made of it.

As with the pitcher in baseball, the server should keep the opponent off-balance by changing the speeds of the serve and by mixing up the flat serve with a spin offering. If this is correctly done, the opponent will frequently hit his service return either too soon and thus into the net; or, he will be late on the return, stroking the ball wide or out of court. Obviously, this will frustrate an opponent.

However, as with the other aspects of tennis, this requires thought and imagination. First, let us consider the flat service. The motion is similar to throwing a ball overhand. In order to hit the ball into the service court, it is important to be aware of two things: 1) the ball must be hit as flatly as possible; and 2) the palm of the hand must go over the ball in order to assure the correct downward angle. Go through the motion using the palm of the hand. Unless the wrist is snapped through, the palm is left pointing upwards, toward the sky. This is also true with a racket, but now the racket face is the palm (of the hand). The server must get the rackethead over the ball to be assured of the desired downward angle, or the serve will fly out of court. Assuming that the toss is correct, but the serve is consistently going into the net, the problem is a smothered serve: the racket is going too far over the ball. Conversely, if the majority of the serves are long and are carrying beyond the service line, the problem is that the rackethead is not going far enough over. More wrist snap should in that case be used.

Should the first serve be a fault, how should the second flat be served? The service motion should be exactly the same as in the first serve, but there should be less wrist snap. The more wrist snap, the greater the speed; but in addition, in order to get the serve into the service area, the ball has to be aimed closer to the top of the net. On the second serve, with less snap used so as to be certain of getting the serve in, the ball can now be aimed higher about the net. This provides a greater safety margin, and enables the server to get the good depth which is so important. Good service depth prevents the opponent from pounding a short second serve, thus taking the offensive thrust of the game away from the server.

Many players hit a hard flat first serve, but those same players hope to push a weak second serve on the net, lacking motion of follow-through, both of which are essential to gain depth and control. An alert opponent pounces on a weak serve either putting it away or hitting such a forceful shot that he is assured of a weak return, which he can then put away and thus win the point.

Invariably, when world class players are asked which shot concerns them the most, the answer is: "getting the good depth and control required for the second service." Relatively speaking, the same concern applies to all tennis players.

The motion of the second serve should not be changed. Everything remains the same: the palm is over the ball, but there is less wrist snap. Less snap enables the server to clear the net by a greater margin. A reasonable pace can be maintained without hitting a blooper, but more importantly, the server gains the depth which keeps the opponent from taking drastic liberties with his service return.

Players experience trouble in achieving the spin serve for various reasons, but a principle reason is their inability to understand that in order to impart spin on the serve, they must brush, or get over and around the ball. In executing the spin serve, it is helpful to consider either of the following mental pictures. First, after tossing the ball, imagine that there is a face on the ball: using the racket as a comb, sweep over the face and brush the hair. This will help the server to get considerable spin and little pace. Should more pace be desired but less spin, brush or hit from the right eye upwards. The server is still brushing the ball, but not as lightly, thus effecting less spin and more pace. The service motion is unchanged; the portion of the face and head that is struck varies with the amount of spin and pace desired.

Another analogy is to picture the ball as being enclosed by a four-cornered diamond. Striking the right corner of the diamond and continuing the service swing will give the serve the desired spin service. By hitting deeper into the diamond, more power and less pace will be provided; and by

Note how vigorously the wrist has snapped through.

just nicking the corner of the diamond, the server will achieve a reverse effect—a considerable amount of spin but reduced velocity.

After learning to serve with spin, players often pose the question: "I can get the spin all right, but the ball keeps going into the net. Why is that and how can it be corrected?" Let us use another baseball analogy. Through judgment and practice, the baseball pitcher can determine how much his curveball curves and drops. The more spin applied, the more the ball curves and the greater the drop. Despite the curving and dropping of the ball, the pitcher is able to hit his target, the catcher's mitt. In the same way, the server can learn to hit the target in the service court area. Through trial and error, decide how much the serve curves and drops, determined by the amount of spin applied to the ball. Hypothetically, let us assume that the serve drops six feet and curves four feet. As the serve is hit, have a mental image of a line six feet about the net. This imaginary line is what the server is to aim for.

Put the ball into the air at a given pace and let the spin pull the ball into the service court. Psychological pressure is considerably lessened, because once the ball has been put six feet above the net, the job is done: the spin will complete the task.

Obviously, the server must also allow for the amount of curve as well as drop on the ball. By aiming a little higher, the server can "walk" the ball deeper into the service area. However, the baseball pitcher does not acquire control without practice, and neither can the server gain control without working at it.

As with the other facets of tennis, depth and control in the service are more important than pace. Once those have been mastered, more pace can be added to the serve.

The service is complex and difficult, but it offers the player absolute command of the moment. The opponent has to await the server's move and can only guess as to the kind of serve to expect as well as the pace and direction. The service is the important offensive weapon. Only through practice can a player hone it to a sharp edge.

HIGH VELOCITY SERVE

By

Dr. M.L. Johnson
Southeastern Louisiana University

Most singles tennis matches are won or lost with the serve. The server has the considerable advantage of being about to toss the ball overhead and strike it with full velocity into the opponent's court. A player should be able to win his own service. If service is broken once, the breaking player needs only to hold his own service in order to win the match. Matching two tournament caliber players, one with an accurate 130 m.p.h. serve would produce odds favoring the higher service velocity.

Every normal person should be able to develop a relatively high velocity serve because he has the mechanical capability. Yet, both amateurs and professionals have problems in reaching their full service velocity potential. The problem is not resolved through reading articles written by players or coaches. A number of publications offer good descriptions of the serve, but the real key to good serving is completely omitted. Since most of the racket head velocity is developed from within the forearm, the difference between high and low velocity serves lies in the effective application of forearm mechanics.

The serve is a series of body movements that start with the larger muscles and sequentially trail out to the smallest muscle groups. A gross mechanical description of the American twist serve is as follows: Grasp the racket diagonally across at the butt of the handle. Diagram 1 shows the proper angles between the racket and the forearm. The player faces the dominant-side net pole. Most of the body weight is initially placed on the dominant-side foot. Toss the ball back into a cocked position where the racket is parallel down the spinal column. The first forward movement is started with the large spinal rotator muscles swinging the pelvis around. Second, the shoulder girdle initiates forward rotation of the flexed arm, closely followed by a complete arm extension to a straight finish with the arm and racket

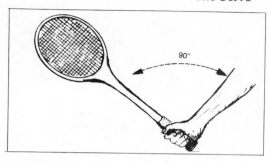

Diagram 1

relatively overhead. Lines 11 through 17 show the shoulder rotation and arm extension sequence (Diagram 2). Finally, the racket is swung around vigorously in a 180° arc by rotating the forearm. Lines Nos. 17-23 show a complete forearm rotation. The acceleration shown in lines 11 through 20 is absorbed by the deceleration shown in lines 21 through 35 (Diagram 2).

Hitting high velocity serves has been shrouded in mystery and opinion in the past because the action takes place so fast. In order to determine what is actually being done, some form of high-speed photography must be used. Diagram 2 shows a composite of pictures made from photographing a world class tennis player. A camera speed of at least 128 frames per second is necessary to isolate sequential movements. Each line represents the frame number of the film sequence. Only the critical zone of lines 11 through 35 are shown in the diagram. Some frames at the beginning and end were omitted from the drawing because the initial and ending movements were relatively slow. Scientific analysis of the serve by high-speed photography leaves little room for opinion about how a particular type of serve should be executed.

The gross mechanical analysis of the preceding paragraph described the American twist serve from start to finish. But, the specific mechanics that make the big difference in serving need further description. The critical factors in stroke execution are as follows: 1) Cocking—using a long arc of swing. 2) Swing—rotating and straightening the arm just prior to racket and ball contact, and 3) Pronation—a vigorous inward rotation of the forearm to swing the racket into the ball.

Cocking—Two things are important in cocking the racket into a position where it is ready to be moved forward. First, the racket must be gripped straight with the palm and fingers straight across the handle. An across-grip is the only way to use effectively the forearm rotation mechanics that produce most of the ball velocity. Second, after the toss, the racket must be positioned vertically down the spinal column. The arm must be fully flexed, with the elbow pointing forward and upward. Similarity between the fully cocked serving position and the cocked position of a baseball pitcher or football passer should be obvious.

Diagram 2

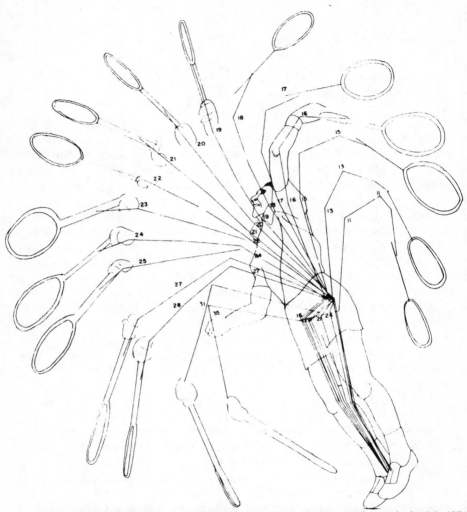

Stanley Plagenhoef, *Patterns of Human Motion:* **a cinematographic analysis (c) 1971. Reprinted by permission of Prentice-Hall, Inc., Englewood Cliffs, New Jersey.**

Swing—Catapulting the racket head into the ball involves timing the sequence of muscle action, and lengthening the racket arm to full extension overhead. As pointed out in the gross analysis, the movement sequence must be from large muscles to small muscles. The fully cocked racket arm is in a position with the elbow pointing upward and forward. Movements from lines 11 through 16 show the shoulder being moved forward and the entire arm being rotated forward. The arm is extended entirely from lines 15 through 18. Sequence lines of the upswing clearly show the principle of using large muscle groups to accelerate the racket. Notice how the elbow is moved up and forward from lines 11 through 17. The hand is also moved rapidly upward and forward until line 18. The upward and forward movement occurs in a very flat arc because the arm is being rotated and quickly extended. At the height of the upward swing forward movement of the arm is slowed. Deceleration of the arm shown by the relative distance between lines 18 and those following enables the racket to be shipped overhead with tremendous acceleration. Relative slowing of a body segment increases the relative velocity of the next body segment. Therefore, rapid initial acceleration of the arm is slowed when the racket is overhead to force subsequent rapid acceleration of the racket head. Also, full extension of the arm at ball contact tends to reduce the amount of angular error in the serve.

Pronation—This is the inward rotation of a body part. Pronation of the forearm near the apex of the stroke provides most of the propulsion for the serve. As shown in lines 17 through 19, the forearm is rotated quickly to swing the racket around fast. The hand is still moving forward in lines 17 through 19, but the racket is being rotated very fast through a complete 180° arc. Preparatory movements from lines 11 through 17 are relatively slow as compared to the fast pronation movement shown in lines 17 through 19.

The movement time for the 180° rotation of the forearm in the tennis serve is only about 3/128 to 5/128 of a second. Thus, most of the racket hand velocity should be derived from an inward rotation of the forearm at the top of the service stroke. There is great similarity between the serve mechanics, and both the javelin throw and an inward breaking curve baseball pitch.

The serving action of a world class tennis player is so fast that the human eye cannot discern the individual movement components. Considerable speculation has been made as to how a high velocity serve is executed. Most of the tennis professionals and authors have described the slow preparatory and ending deceleration movement in detail, with only superficial reference to wrist snap at the height of the swing. Mechanical analysis of the world class tennis player clearly shows no wrist snap. Instead, the critical action is shown to be a vigorous inward rotation of the forearm. Thus, the well-kept secret of executing a high velocity American twist serve lies in a timed sequence of arm movements culminating with rotation of the forearm at the apex of the stroke. Preliminary trunk rotation is used to initiate serving movements. Throwing the racket head quickly upward and forward, and rotating the forearm rapidly at the height of the swing produces the high velocity serves of Conners, Tanner, and Newcomb.

4 THE VOLLEY

THE VOLLEY

By

Paul Assaiante

The definition of a volley is a stroke in which the ball is hit before it has bounced. In order to hit a volley, a person must be standing inside the court boundaries because if he were not, he would be hitting an "out" ball. The volley stroke is truly one of the most important in the game because the purpose of moving to the net to make a volley is to score a placement, or to force the opponent into an error. Moving to the net in an effort to hit a volley places tremendous pressure on your opponent. Even if the opponent has sound ground strokes, the pressure caused by your presence at the net will often cause an error. When rallying from the baseline, your goal is to move the ball around and to hit the proper percentage shots, but, when you move to the net, you force your opponent to hit a non-percentage shot. Anytime you can do this the odds will lean heavily in your favor to win the point. That is, of course, only if you are fairly proficient at executing the volley stroke. Now that we understand the importance of having a volley stroke in your stroke repertoire, let us examine the mechanics of its execution.

The continental grip is the best grip to use when volleying because it requires no switch of grips. During a fast exchange at the net, it is virtually impossible to accurately switch grips because of the very short time that you have to prepare. When volleying, a good player is able to hit volleys with the same grip off either side by using the opposite face of the racket.

It is important to keep in mind that there is no independent movement of the wrist during a volley. Your arm, wrist and racket head should come through the ball as a unit and this can only occur properly if your wrist is firm.

Your preparation, or backswing, must be very short because you will find yourself hitting the ball too late if you take a big backswing. A large preparation will also usually cause a long follow through which will hurt your chances of recovering from the shot, regaining a balanced ready position before the next one. For a normal, waist high volley, the racket should not be taken back any further than your shoulder. Your goal when volleying is to meet the ball as early as possible which should be in front of your body. One way to accomplish this is to have a very short backswing, while the other way is to make contact with the ball with a straightened arm. Straightening the hitting arm is probably the simplest way to give you a sense of the punching action utilized during the volley.

Attempt to pivot your upper body as you swing your racket back during the preparation phase of the volley. Step diagonally towards the oncoming ball while at the same time bringing your racket forward to meet the ball as early in its path as you possibly can. Although this whole process sounds remarkably easy, it is incredible how few people spend the time needed to perfect this type of stroke.

There are several different types of volleys that you need to learn how to execute if you are going to be successful at net play. Some of these will be forced upon you by your opponent, while some you will be able to force your opponents to produce for you.

The high volley gives many intermediates and beginners great difficulty because they tend to overswing in an attempt to kill the ball. This happens because the ball is moving towards you fairly slowly (if it were moving rapidly at this height, it would probably sail over the baseline and you would be wise to let it go by). You should, however, go for a fairly offensive volley on a high ball by driving it deep to the open corner of the court. One word of caution on this shot—your racket should be slightly closed so as to prevent the ball from sailing long. A closed racket face would be facing slightly towards the ground as opposed to an open racket face which would be facing slightly skyward.

On a low volley, or one which you must execute from a position lower than your waist, you must be very careful not to try to hit a winner. The nature of this ball has forced you into a neutral position and, as a result, you cannot hit an offensive shot. You must bend your knees in an attempt to get as close to the ball as possible. You must also concentrate on keeping your wrist on the same level as your racket head which will produce a natural underspin on this low ball.

For balls hit directly at you, or reflex volleys, just attempt to get a firm racket in front of the ball. This is not an offensive situation, but as long as the racket is held firmly, you should be able to get the ball over the net in an effective manner.

A weak volleyer fears net play and the speed at which the ball is moving when he is at the net. The only way to overcome this fear is to spend many hours positioned at the net hitting volley after volley. When you are in this position, avoid taking too big a swing while concentrating on keeping your arm straight. Do not be overly concerned with underspin because being

Photos #1-13 demonstrate correct volley skills. Photo #1 shows the proper ready position for a player at the net. The continental grip should be used, and the racket head should be "tilted up" slightly. This allows for a more rapid racket movement during the execution of the volley. Photo #2 illustrates the proper body position for a low volley. The knees are bent, the body is balanced (weight-wise), and the racket head is always kept higher than the wrist. Photos 3-6 show how to execute a backhand volley. The racket arm on the backhand volley should be straight and the free hand should cradle the throat of the racket up until the time the racket begins its forward movement towards the ball. This action causes the player to feel like he is "shooting a sling shot" and is the impetus that gives "sting" to the volley. The weight should be transferred on to the foot closest to the net. The wrist should be firm throughout the stroke.

7 8

9 10

Photos #7-10 illustrate how to hit a forehand volley. The racket arm should be comfortably flexed in order to keep the player from being "crowded" by the ball. The stroking motion should be kept quite short in order to ensure that contact is made in front of the body. Again, the wrist should be kept firm. Make sure that your shoulders are turned so that volleys can be hit down the line, as well as crosscourt. Photos #11-13 show the "don'ts" of volleying:

#11. Don't let the racket head drop below your wrist.

#12. Don't take too big a swing.

#13. Don't let the elbow lead.

11

12

13

THE DON'TS OF VOLLEYING
#11. Don't let rackethead drop below your wrist.
#12. Don't take too big a swing.
#13. Don't let elbow lead.

obsessed with it will cause a chopping motion. The continental grip will impart natural underspin on the ball. Make sure that your racket head does not drop lower than your wrist and also that you attempt to recover to a good ready position regardless of whether you think that you have hit a winner or not.

THE VOLLEY

By

James H. Leighton Jr.
Presbyterian College

To examine the volley we have asked a panel of experts for their opinions. The panel consists of Jack Kramer, Helen Jacobs, Don Budge, Bill Tilden, and teaching professional, Lloyd Budge.

There is certainly a great deal more to the volley than the technique or execution of the shot. Since preparation and position are important in any discussion of this department of the game, they are included in this article.

JACK KRAMER—Execution: A long stroke should not be used. The volley may be compared to a short punch in boxing or a quick kick in football. There should be almost no follow-through. A player should keep his racket head high, hit with a downward motion, and use a brushing stroke to get underspin. His wrist must be firm, and he should complete the stroke as quickly as possible. He should start with a very short backswing. Timing, balance, and keeping the eyes on the ball are outstanding factors in the success of this shot. In a low shot, backswing and follow-through are at a minimum. The low volley is a defensive shot, and a slight undercut or slice is necessary in order to execute it effectively. The speed with which the stroke is made may frequently cause a player to violate the stance rule about keeping his body sideways to the net. In the backhand, a player's thumb controls the racket. The racket should be raised to the player's left shoulder. At the moment of impact, a slight undercut of the ball should be made. The player's feet should be spread apart about two feet, and his body weight should be distributed equally. The follow-through is to the right and upward. On the low backhand, there is a slight follow-through.

Preparation: A wise player will attempt to pace his attack so that he will be in the proper position as much of the time as is possible. The player should keep moving in, and once he starts in, he should not hesitate.

Position: A player must play as close to the net as possible without placing himself in danger of having a lob sent over his head. Of course, a fast player can advance closer than a slow man, since he is able to race back faster to recover lobs. The players should not go into the center of the net. If he sends a forcing shot deep to his opponent's backhand, he can anticipate a cross-court return, but he must guard against his opponent passing him down the line. For that reason, he will go in a bit to the right side of the net. Position in practicing the volley should be 10 to 12 feet from the net.

Comments: Jack Kramer does a good job of describing the speed of the volley. However, it is probably wise to avoid calling it a stroke. One of the main reasons a player misses volleys is because he does too much with the racket. The racket motion should be kept in as short an area as is possible, particularly in the case of beginners and those players who are trying to acquire a mechanical type of volley. Watching the ball cannot be overemphasized. The volley is the kill and its finality brings an anxiety which makes a player want to look where the ball is going rather than at it, or before that moment, to look for the opening.

Regarding preparation, Kramer says, once he starts in, he should not hesitate. This point should be brought out in two ways. First of all, once a player has recognized a ball as one he should go in on, then he should go right on through it without stopping at the point of hitting the ball. His feet should be moving while he is hitting. From that point to the time when the opponent is about to make his shot, the feet of the player who is volleying should be similar to greased lightning, taking him into position. Without this combination, it is impossible for a player to be in the proper position for the volley.

The main thing to keep in mind is that a player should generally tend to bisect the angle formed by his opponent's possible returns. Kramer's advice to practice well back from the net is good. Any tennis player can make a volley on top of the net.

HELEN JACOBS—Execution: The principles of footwork, body balance, and weight shifting which are the essence of good ground strokes also apply to the volley, although there are times when the rapid flight of the ball allows a player to do nothing more than throw his weight into the shot. The backswing is the same as that used for the forehand or backhand drive except that it is shorter. When a player hits a ball at close range or low, he uses only the slightest backswing. In this case, the action is more blocking than it is stroking. When the ball comes to a player above the net, the backswing should be lengthened in order to get more power. As the player brings the racket forward, a shift of weight takes place. At the end of the backswing the player's wrist should be bent back, in line with his rear shoulder. In the volley, his shoulders do not turn as far around as they do in the ground strokes.

On the forward swing, his wrist straightens out to lock at the moment of impact, but does not remain locked as it does in the drive. A continuation of the wrist's forward movement adds punch to the volley. The follow-through is short, ending on a backhand when the player's arm is fully extended. When the volley is blocked or when a player thrusts at the ball with his forearm and locked wrist, the racket continues in line with the direction of the ball for just a short distance, perhaps two feet in front of him. In all volleys, it is the turning of the shoulders toward the net and their forward thrust which assists the player's arm and wrist in giving force to the shot. A flat volley which is made with the racket head parallel to the ground is the most punishing. Occasionally, on a ball well above the net, a slight overspin is useful. Sometimes a ball that is well below the net can be volleyed more safely with a slight underspin.

Preparation: No preparation is necessary.

Position: When practicing, a player should stand midway between the net and the service line. In going in behind a forcing drive, the player should stand closer.

Comments: It is true that a player's shoulders do not always come around on the volley as much as they do for the ground strokes, but it is important to make a considerable turn and not volley while facing the net. The shoulders certainly do not rotate forward as they do in the ground strokes. This statement is particularly true in the case of straight volleys. In fact, on the backhand volley, many times it is advisable to let the left hand go back as the ball is contacted. This movement is used for balance and for preventing a turn of the shoulders. On the forehand volley, the left hand will cross backward and underneath the right as the volley is made. However, a player's shoulders should be thrust forward into the shot.

It should be kept in mind that the volley is not made with the player's whole arm and his shoulder, but rather with his forearm and wrist, or from his elbow to the racket tip.

If a player is having difficulty with his timing, the following exercises may be of assistance: On the forehand, the coach should stress his contacting the ground with his left foot at the same time that the racket contacts the ball. On the backhand the right foot would be used. This exercise will emphasize stepping into the ball and will give the player a sense of the weight shift receiving much of the speed of the ball rather than racket work which is overdone.

Once again, it is important not to talk about a backswing on the volley. Regarding Miss Jacobs' remark that the racket should be parallel to the ground on the flat volley, parallel is incorrect; it should be perpendicular.

Miss Jacobs is sound in her views on the use of the player's wrist in the volley. It should be cocked upward and backward, moved downward into the ball, locked firmly at impact, and then continued down underneath the ball imparting underspin. This particular action of the player's wrist will give safety to the shot and add speed. Of course, it is used for what might be termed a sliced type of volley. This type of volleying can be described loosely as though a player were digging a hole in the court at a point just ahead of the ball. Also, this action is more applicable to balls of average height than it is to low or high ones. The former should either be blocked with a semi-open face, opening somewhat at contact to raise the ball and for spin, or should be made with a completely open face at the start, with the racket sliding underneath the ball as it carries the ball into court. Probably the high balls should be blocked more frequently than is suggested by the experts.

DON BUDGE — Execution: In preparing to receive the ball for a volley, a player should take a stance facing the net. When he is in this position, he is prepared to move either to the right or to the left. The weight of his body goes into making the volley; he makes a side turn to facilitate the transfer of his weight forward. Often it is necessary to hit facing, but the player's weight should be behind the shot. As a rule, the backswing does not go much farther than the player's rear shoulder. On low balls the backswing and the follow-through are negligible; on high balls a player can get more punch. A kill or a drive volley can be used on high balls. On the kill volley we start our backswing with the same loop that is used in the forehand drive, but bring it down on the ball from the height of the loop. The impact is made with an open face racket; the ball is hit flat. Whether a player uses a long or short backswing, the ball should be met well in front, as high as possible.

The head of the racket should always be above the player's wrist except on low balls. He can keep it above his wrist on some low balls by stooping down to the ball. The wrist should be bent slightly as the racket is carried back, but it straightens out in alignment with the player's arm as the racket is brought against the ball. It is locked stiff at the moment of contact, thus bracing the racket against the impact of a ball taken in full flight. Additional punch is supplied to a volley by the action of the forearm and the reinforcement of the shoulder. The majority of volleys are hit either flat or with a slight underspin. On volleys taken above the level of the net, a little overspin can be used. We prefer to hit the ball flat, using a forward bevel of the bottom edge for those much above the level of the net.

Preparation: A player should not go in on a drive he hits from behind the baseline. He should wait for his opponent to give him a short ball. It is important that he get in swiftly all the way, and his approach must have good depth and pace. In case of a lob, he should be prepared to check momentum. The risk in going to the net lies in a player's approach at the wrong time on a weak drive, and in his failure to go in fast enough or in being trapped by a lob.

Position: A player should station himself at the center of the net except at times when his drive has forced the opponent so wide that part of the court is closed off to his return. When a player is wide, he should cover more to that side.

The Volley

Comments: A great deal of this description pertains to the drive type of volley and is better left to players of the caliber of Don Budge than to the average player. More volleys are missed by doing too much rather than too little, and this point should be stressed constantly.

Few players get low enough for the low volleys, and they cannot be made properly without a player being down low to the ball. Here, even more than on the ground strokes, the knees should be used as an elevator to take a player down to the proper level.

Budge's comments on preparation are very good. Players often come in from too far back only to find that they have to make a low defensive volley. The short ball is the one to come in on, and waiting for it will pay off in easy kills. There is little point in a player piling into the net continuously only to find he has to defend. The volley should be the culmination of a well-planned attack.

BILL TILDEN—Execution: The foot that is away from the ball steps directly across toward the opposite sideline. In case of a ball directly at a player, he should step backward with the foot closest to the ball on the side he wishes to play. He should swing that foot back and behind him toward the opposite sideline. If there is not time to change feet, he should throw his weight on the foot that is closest to the ball and lean in. The racket head should be lifted above his wrist with a very short backswing. Move the racket head forward into the line of flight of the oncoming ball and meet it flat with a stiff wrist about six to ten inches closer to the net than the foremost line of the body. The player should block the ball directly to where he wants it to go and above all, he should not follow through. Volley gains its power from an opponent's shot, plus the solidity of the player's block and stiff wrist. On all volleys the racket head should be above the player's wrist at the moment of meeting the ball. A player should not let the ball come to him. He should go out with his racket and meet it on the way.

Preparation: The advance to the net should always be made after careful, proper preparation when an opponent has been placed on the defensive and when the chances of making a winning shot are better than 50-50. A player should never go to the net just because someone has said it should invariably be done. He should go in when his own intelligence directs because he has worked up the attack to that point. Go to the net for only one reason—to win a point outright with a kill. Never defend at the net. Prepare to volley on the way in. The racket should be carried with the head up in front of the player. His advancing shot must have depth and power.

Position: The correct volley position is six to ten feet from the net and about two or three feet to the center side of a straight line, drawn from the point the opponent is hitting his shot straight down the player's court parallel to the sidelines. At the net a player seldom has more than two-thirds of his court to cover. The straight third is in front of a cross court which an opponent can hit into with little risk. The remaining third is on the extreme side of the court away from the ball, and is so difficult to hit into with a passing shot which clears the net, that a player can afford to give his opponents few winning shots. In coming to the net from the back court, a player should always follow the line of his shot, but stay just to the center side of it. In coming to the net, do not hit down center, but definitely into a corner of the court, or on a sharp angle.

Comments: Tilden is more precise in his statements about hitting the ball out front than the others—about six to ten inches closer to the net than the foremost line of the body—and in doing so highlights this all-important feature of the volley. He should go out with his racket and meet it on the way.

Preparation for the volley on the way in is also important. The player who goes in with his racket well in front and up will be able to line it up, pause, and make the volley with ease and finality.

In the volley, flexibility of footwork and racket work are more important than they are in other phases of the game. Tilden brings out this point regarding footwork when he talks about the handling of a close ball. Rather than have the foot closest to the ball going back and behind, it is better to talk in terms of diagonal footwork. For instance on the forehand volley, the player's left foot would go forward, but toward the left sideline. In this way, his body will be out of the way, but he will be able to get his weight into the shot.

Tilden is the only one of our group who does not advise the player to follow through. Some follow-through is certainly permissible and Helen Jacobs' suggestion of two feet is not too far, but for beginners and in situations where a player has to make a volley, Tilden's advice is particularly sound. It is also sound on all difficult volleys.

LLOYD BUDGE—Execution: The racket head should be drawn back only about a foot beyond the intended point of impact with the ball. It points slightly over the player's right shoulder at an angle halfway in between the straight up and down vertical position of the serve and the straight out horizontal position of the forehand drive. The player's wrist should be bent back slightly and without complete flexibility of the ground stroke. Rigidity as the ball meets the racket is one of the prime objectives in making a volley. From a slightly bent back position, the racket should be brought forward to meet the ball as far out in front of the body as possible. Although it is better to get sideways to the net, it is not necessary. As the racket comes forward to meet the ball, the shot is probably best described as an attempt to block the ball back over the net. The player's wrist is tightened and locked as the racket meets the ball, and the follow-through is being cut very short. During this stroke the player's elbow should be bent in towards his body and his wrist should be well below the racket head. In making the volley, the bevel of the racket should be slightly open with the lower edge of the racket an inch or two forward from the top edge. On a slow ball the racket can be drawn back quite a bit further, and the wrist can be made more flexible in its backswing. The same lock of the wrist is necessary at the moment of impact, but the player can get extra speed in the shot by drawing the strings of his racket sharply under the ball as he meets it and continuing his follow-through forward and under.

Comments: Lloyd Budge, as well as most of the other experts, suggests that the player's wrist be bent back slightly. Volleying is a thing of finesse, touch, and delicacy. It is the movement of the racket into the ball through the wrist which provides a considerable amount of these qualities.

Budge describes the volley as a block. Actually, there are two schools of thought on the volley. We can divide them into blockers and punchers.

Blockers will generally use the standard Eastern forehand and backhand grips. Their volleys are usually hit close to them and they give the appearance of defending themselves with their rackets. They usually hit the ball with a flat racket and their action is somewhat similar to that of the chip shot in golf.

The punchers hit the ball with a more open face and as though they were digging a hole in the court just ahead of contact. They hit it well away from them and probably use more wrist than do the blockers. Their hit is a slice. A case can be built for the fact that most of the players who are most proficient in the volley come into this category, but either method is sound and a case can also be built for the players who are able to volley both ways.

It would be wise to note Budge's: The player's elbow should be bent in towards his body. This is particularly true of the blocking type of volley, but it should be kept in mind that there is a small amount of inside-out motion (the elbow going away from the body) in the volley as there is in the ground strokes. This motion can only come about when the elbow is in close.

Not one of our experts has talked about where to hit the volley and something should be added about that. Of course, we can start on the general principle that it should be hit to a weakness. However, beginners should be instructed to get the deep cross-court volleys down fast. Next, the angles cross-court volleys should be added, and then the players will be using more of the court. Finally, the straight volleys should be added. In stating this order, we are not talking about the importance of a particular direction because nothing is more important than the straight volley which closes off the court to the opponent as it does. Rather, we are talking about the students making the shots that are safest for them. Nothing is more discouraging than building up an opening and then missing the volley. It might be added here that carelessness can be the cause of most missed volleys. Good players never miss an easy volley.

Occasionally, it is advisable to fake at the net. Give the opponent an opening and then cover it fast once he has committed himself, and always tend to leave this opening on the side on which the opponent's passing shots are the poorest.

The Volley

A player should volley as close to the net as he can and still handle a lob, but the lob must be discounted somewhat unless the opponent is a capable lobber. If the player is in close, he should make the volley stationary, particularly if it is a straight one. If a player is volleying cross-court he will have to be moving over somewhat as he makes it to get into position to cover the down-the-line shot. However, if he is volleying from a back position, he should move through the shot as he makes it. Position is everything at the net once a player has become proficient in volleying.

On coming in, no mention has been made of the center theory, that is, hitting the coming-in shot deep into the center of the court. This shot should be used from time to time, particularly against big swingers and players who have good cross-court passing shots. A player will be cutting down his opponent's angle when the coming-in shot is hit deep into the center of the court. It should be remembered that most short balls along the player's sidelines should be hit deep down the adjacent sideline.

Above all, never miss a coming-in shot. At a point when a player has his opponent where he wants him, the opponent has given the player the short ball he has been waiting for. Now the player should move carefully, but surely, and give the opponent an opportunity to make the error or hit the ball he can volley away.

A few more points should be added on the coming-in shot. A player should come in behind sliced shots, particularly on low balls. They are usually safer. This action is sometimes called chipping the ball into court. When it is necessary to come in from some distance back, a player should come in under a slow slice. This action gives him time to get into position. The coach should instruct his students to come behind their serves. They may find themselves volleying up continuously. It is better to draw the short return and come in on that. Certainly coming in behind the second serve should be tempered.

Position is everything at the net once a player has become proficient in volleying.

IMPROVE YOUR NET PROFIT

By

Vandy Christie
Northwestern University

A tennis court is 78 feet long: 39 feet, of course, from the net to each baseline. It is logical that one sound way to win a large percentage of points lies in the player's ability to get to the net. Thus, if a player learns when, where and how to play at the net, his or her winning percentage will skyrocket! Our purpose here is to point out the footwork and basic hitting position which should be used when playing at the net. The teacher and student must deal carefully with when to go and how to proceed with proper footwork and controlled court movement.

Preparation: As the player sets up for hitting the ball (Illustration A1), the racket should be held in front, ready to go to the left or right. The player should be slightly bent at the waist, with the weight forward and ready to sping from the front part of the feet—on the toes! After serving or hitting an approach shot, the player is already positioned at the net. In the illustration, Jeff is well prepared for the next move. He has just come to a stop with a split-step, thus winding up in the position shown. In preparing for the stroke, the player should keep the head up and be on the toes.

The Stroke: Before explaining the actual forehand and backhand, proper footwork when entering into the stroke will be discussed. Ideally, we want our players to step toward the net post with the outside foot. The outside foot for a right-handed player is the left foot on the forehand and the right foot on the backhand side. The player stepping toward the net post (on the right for a forehand) will be on a diagonal and will therefore be stepping into the ball. This crossover step will help to direct the return, and by being on the toes, the player can make the step and be successful. Often there will be no time for such a quick step—the player will be much closer to the opponent. In these cases, it is necessary to reach out, as shown in Illustration A2. Concentrate on the step, however, in order to avoid hitting across the ball while pulling back to the position; the ball in this case has side spin, and the player's percentage will drop. Be alert, be active, and think about the feet.

Illustration A-1

Illustration A-2

Illustration A-3

Illustration A-4

The Volley

Illustration B-1

Illustration B-2

Illustration B-3

Illustration C-1

Illustration C-2

The Volley

Illustration D-1

Illustration D-2

Illustration D-3

Illustration E-1

Illustration E-2

The Volley

Forehand and Backhand: The purpose of the cross step is to place the player into the position of the aggressor. By coming to the net, the player becomes the aggressor; the point, however, must be completed. In order not to give the impression of laziness, the player must step forward as described when possible; otherwise, this laziness will give points to the opponent. The actual stroke for hitting is quite simple. The racket head is brought back only as far as the shoulder axis. (Draw a line straight out from the point of the shoulder.) Too many big backswings are made at the net; there is not time to do this. A simple backswing should be used. Strike the ball in front of the body, with the hitting arm extended, and using very little follow-through. In Series B, Jeff is hitting a fairly good backhand volley. Our players learn to strike the ball when it is in front of them, and not to break their wrists at the point of impact. The wrist should be kept fairly still; the player will want to hit a touch volley, or put some slice on it, but that should be saved for later. In the meantime, note how some slice is applied to the ball on the forehand in Series C, and note how well the player is stepping.

Because racket action is so important to a successful shot, the head of the racket should be kept steady. In Series D, note the head of the racket of Jeff goes for a wide backhand. There is not follow-through after he hits the ball; the footwork is good because he is late and must catch the ball. The actual hitting stroke should not be more than a three-foot motion. The racket, in other words, should not move more than the distance from the backswing (shoulder line) to the hit, and with a limited follow-through.

When returning a ball hit directly at the player, efficiency of motion is the key. The baseline is not a bad place from which to hit to the opponent at the net; hit it directly at the opponent. In Series E, Jeff does not overreact: he stays in one place and gets his racket on the ball. Economize the motion! Remain in place and concentrate on hitting the ball by blocking the ball in front of the body, if possible.

Our players learn that they must choose their opportunities to go to the net, but they also know that the points can be won there and that the match can be controlled from the net. We like for them to be close on the net when possible, cutting off passing shots and finishing off the points. Too many good players merely pop the ball back to the opponent, and do not concentrate on putting the ball and the opponent away. Finally, concentrate, watch the ball, stay on the toes, think about each point, and net profits will improve.

FAILURE TO WATCH THE BALL- PARTICULARLY THE VOLLEY

By

Vince Eldred
Tennis Professional

Mistakes which result from failure to watch the ball are hitting too soon, hitting too late, hitting the ball where it is instead of blocking/punching the volley. An additional mistake seems to be more psychological than anything else. A volleyer's serves become sluggish due to the fact that he is not aware that the ball does not have to travel the same distance as it does when he is on the baseline. The preceding statement would seem to be obvious, but players do not seem to realize this fact.

Concentration, as in any athletic endeavor, is of paramount importance. Conversely, a lapse of concentration is disastrous. If it is conceded that the first two statements are true, it would follow that watching the ball requires concentration. Timing is also closely allied with concentration. To execute any shot successfully, the components—watching the ball, timing, and concentration—are necessary. The volley is no exception.

Following the ball, visually, into the racket strings is the ideal. Actually, what the player is really doing is projecting his eyes ahead of the airborne ball. Should he hit the ball where it is now, he would miss it. Once it is determined when and where he will hit the ball, action and relexes, in that split second, take over. It is similar to skeet shooting. The shooter is not aiming and shooting at the point where the clay pigeon is now. He is leading the bird and firing at the point where the bird will be a split second later. This analogy is applicable to the volleyer in tennis.

Through time spent in observing and teaching tennis, we have found that players do not watch the ball long enough. They pull the trigger too soon. They are too anxious. They either want to see where the ball is going or the whereabouts of their opponent.

The Volley

It is safe to say, the better the player, the longer he watches the ball approaching the contact point, racket meeting ball, before shifting his eyes to the target area where he is aiming.

The beginner or intermediate player, takes his eyes off the ball to see where it is going considerably sooner than does the good tennis player. The less talented individual spends less time watching the ball than the better player.

Some people may be of the opinion that a tennis player becomes conditioned to watching the ball and concentration plays a small part. We disagree. In our opinion, there is a definite correlation between concentration, timing which is linked to concentration on the ball is one of the contributing factors to excellence.

Without dwelling on the indefinite number of reasons why some players are better than their counterparts, we feel that the poorest player, assuming he is physically fit and has hand/eye coordination, can watch the ball longer by using concentration.

Consider a few rules or mental pictures. As the ball is approaching, try to concentrate on reading the label on it, or look for the seams on the ball. Very few, if any tennis players are endowed with vision good enough to perceive the manufacturer's label or pick up the seams on a ball in flight. This is something for a player to concentrate on while getting ready to hit the ball. If it helps him focus on the hitting point so much the better.

The average player tends to watch the ball less when volleying at the net than in hitting a conventional groundstroke from the baseline area. Why? At first glance, the volley appears to be, is or should be an easier shot to execute than a forehand or backhand. Due to the fact that the player is closer to the net, that barrier becomes less of a problem than a groundstroke. Along this line of thought, the player is lulled into a false sense of complacency.

When he is at the net, a player should think of himself as a boxer. On the baseline he is fighting long range. Once he moves into the net, the infighting starts. The infighter uses shorter punches. Therefore, the volleyer should shorten his backswing and punch/block the ball. Usually, before the ball is within punching distance, some players lift their eyes and look at the point where they are aiming instead of zeroing in on the ball. The result is that the ball is hit off-center on the racket, sometimes hitting the frames and ricochets out of court. If it is returned, the opposition has an easy kill.

In our opinion, the volleyer has a good chance of psyching himself favorably by considering the following approach. When he is at the net, the ball has less distance to travel, and that can only mean he has to watch it closely. He must get ready faster, shorten his backswing, and block the ball in front or it will be past him before he can swing. He should watch the ball right into his racket. It is going faster, relatively speaking, because of volleyer is closer to the ball when his opponent hits it. If anything, he should watch the ball closer than when he is in the backcourt. He must realize that his eyes have to be alert, and project ahead faster than they do when he is on the baseline. In addition, there is not bounce, which gives him additional time.

If a player thinks about these suggestions or along similar lines, he will have something other than physical reflexes to aid him. Along with the physical, he also has intellectual help. Watching the ball in all phases of tennis, but in this instance volleying, boils down to intense concentration.

To some extent, a player may be conditioned to keep his eyes on the ball; however, concentration plays a larger role. Attentiveness, along with intellectual guidelines, geared to concentration, should help to make the player's next volley a good one.

Note the excellent concentration by this player who is stroking a volley.

IMPROVING THE BACKHAND VOLLEY

By

Thomas G. Pucci
University of Arkansas

Tennis players of all ages and abilities often seem to have trouble with the backhand volley. Actually, however, it is one of the simplest strokes in that the swing is brief and uncomplicated. The ball is visible in front of the body throughout the swing.

As with any stroke, the first phase of the backhand volley should be a good ready position. This is accomplished by standing with a slight crouch, with the weight on the balls of the feet. The racket should be grasped lightly at the throat with the hand opposite the player's hitting hand. When the player sees the ball approaching the backhand side, the racket is drawn back with the hand on the racket throat.

As this is happening, the shoulders are pivoting to the side so that the side of the body is facing the net. This motion will bring the racket back in a natural movement. After this phase is completed, the racket is stopped; the racket head is kept cocked above the hand throughout the entire stroke.

When the ball is approaching, the right foot should step into the ball as the racket comes forward to meet the ball with a short punching motion in front of the body. This does not mean swinging wildly at the ball as so many players do when they become excited under the pressures of match competition. What it does mean, is stepping into the ball so that all the weight is transferred into it at point of contact. So often, even at the advanced level, we see a player hitting the backhand volley in back of him or very close to the body with the weight on the back foot.

Another common fault that is often seen is the player stepping into the ball too soon. When this occurs, the player usually hits the volley with just the arm and not the entire body, which is so vital for accuracy and putting the ball away. When this happens, the player will feel no power in the volley and will lob at the ball with a loose wrist. In a sense he has already transferred the weight to the forward foot without moving the upper part of the body. When this occurs, the motion becomes very jerky and a slapping motion results. It is important that the player step into the ball as the racket comes forward, in order to get optimum power and accuracy.

At contact with the ball, the player should have a firm wrist and tight grip so that the racket does not wobble. The racket head should still be held above the hand holding the racket in order to give the shot maximum leverage. The shoulder closest to the net should be pointed down into the shot to make certain that all the body parts are driving into the ball.

Many coaches fail to emphasize the follow-through on the backhand volley. This phase of the stroke production is as important as in any other stroke. After contact is made with the ball, a brief follow-through should be made. The racket should follow through in the direction of the flight of the ball. As the follow-through is completed, the back foot should be brought forward so that a ready position can be again attained and the player is ready for the next shot.

For some reason the high backhand volley seems to give most players trouble. Too often, a coach sees a player miss that easy high backhand volley with the opponent off the court out of position. Again, as in any backhand volley, the ball must be hit out in front of the body. A common error is for the player to let the wrist lag so that the racket head is open. This error will cause the ball to be hit long. The wrist and grip must be firm to avoid this. The player should attack the ball, attempting to keep the racket on the ball as long as possible. He should follow through in the direction the ball is hit.

Coaches often fail to drill players on those easy, high backhand volleys. In many instances matches are lost because a player misses this shot. Constant drill is necessary for this to be corrected. In practice sessions, players must not only work on low volleys, but also on the so-called easy shots.

Any low volley is a most difficult shot. Because the player is very close to the net, he must worry not only about the depth of the shot, but also about getting the ball up quickly to cross the net. We tell our players to get the body low. This means bending the knees and placing the eyes and head at the line of flight of the ball. This movement not only helps the player keep the eyes on the ball, but it also forces him to stay low for the entire shot. It is a common error for the player to drop the racket head to the level of the ball and fail to get the rest of the body at that low level. When this occurs, it results in the player scooping the ball with a weak, wrist motion and not accuracy. The player quickly finds himself on the defense, rather than the desired offense.

The most difficult volley for many players is the ball hit directly at them. The player does not have time to step to one side or the other for the conventional forehand or backhand volley. Many times he cannot attack the ball but has only a very short time to react. All that a player can do in this situation is place the racket in front of the body and hit a blocking backhand volley. If the ball is below the line of the net, the racket must be slanted upward to give the ball lift. There is not room and no time for backswing with this shot; it is strictly a reflex motion. If the wrist is kept firm and the racket held very tightly in the hand, the ball can be met squarely. The player should attempt to lean into the shot as much as possible in order to get the weight into the shot. The racket should be aimed at the spot in the opposite court and the follow-through should be in that direction.

Thus, the backhand volley does not have to be the tennis coach's nightmare as it so often is. Constant drill and practice can make the backhand volley the aggressive winning shot that it should be. The basic points that coaches should emphasize when drilling the players on this shot are the following: 1) a good ready position; 2) racket head should be cocked and held above the hand holding the racket; 3) a firm wrist and grip; 4) the ball should be hit out in front of the body; 5) a short punching stroke should be used; 6) follow-through; 7) watch the ball.

PLAY THE ANGLES

By

C. Jay McWilliams
Hudson High School, Ohio

In order to develop a strong tennis game, the varsity player must learn to handle the shot that comes to him at an angle, and to hit the angle shot from the forehand and the volleying position.

In order to practice handling the deep angled forehand and backhand drive, we use a bombardment drill. Since we do not have a mechanical ball machine, we have developed what we call our human ball machine. We set up four players at one end of the court, behind the baseline. Each of the four players has three tennis balls in hand. Starting from left to right, each player in turn strokes a drive to the single player behind the opposite baseline in the receiving position. The receiver continues to receive drives coming at various angles until a total of 12 balls has been hit. The drill continues until all five players have had an opportunity to receive the 12 angle shots (Diagram 1).

In our next drill the receiver practices handling the shot that comes at an angle. In this drill, we station two players at midcourt who practice volleying shots hit at angles to the center of the court. Either the coach or one of the players stands behind the baseline with 24 tennis balls in a hopper, and hits the balls at varying angles to the midcourt area. The player in the best position returns the shot by using a volleying stroke. The placement of the two players on the court is shown in Diagram 2. The baseline player attempts to hit balls to either midcourt sideline while the other two players attempt to return with a firm volleying stroke.

In practicing our angle volleying we have two drills which have been very effective. In the first drill, the coach or an experienced player is stationed behind the baseline with a hopper of balls. These are used in stroking forehand and backhand drives to three other players stationed across the net in the area where the center line bisects the service line. Diagram 3 illustrates the positions of these three players. When they are stationed just inside the service line, they are in the No. 3 position. The three players move forward, halfway between the service line and the net, into the No. 2 position and the same procedure as above is followed. Finally, they move to the No. 1 position which is just a racket and arm length away from the net, where they will again attempt to angle-volley the shots hit at them by the coach or assistant. A variation of this drill is to use a single player who will volley from positions 1, 2 and 3, using the human ball machine to hit rapid fire shots at the volleyer. The volleyer will either angle the volleys or can hit down the line (Diagram 4).

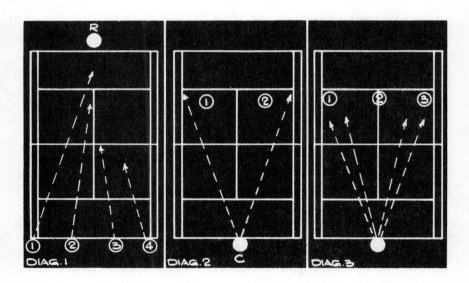

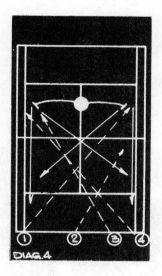

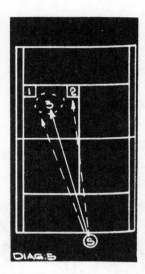

The service is taught using the angled serve. The area designated as area 1 in Diagram 5 is our point of aim. Players usually use a variety of serves, therefore, the emphasis is on placement of the serve with a smooth, fluid motion. Thus, our first choice in placement of the serve is the sideline corner of the service as shown in Diagram 5. The second area to which the players are taught to serve is that area in the inside corner of the service box. The third choice is to serve into the center of the service box, with depth to the serve. Area 3 is recommended for second service, in order to cut down on double faulting.

Angle shots are not the only shots that we practice. The down-the-line shot, drop shot, and offensive and defensive lobs are also emphasized in our practice plans.

To illustrate the variety of shots practiced in our daily workouts, the following pre-practice warm-up plan is followed by all team members. Using our ladder rankings, we select two players who will go through this warm-up. Our format is as follows:

1) Both players hit from behind their respective baseline, both forehand and backhand drives.

2) One player comes to the net while the other remains behind the baseline. They hit for a short period, then reverse positions.

3) Both players come to the net and volley.

4) One player lobs and the other uses the overhead smash; they then reverse positions.

We do not follow the same procedure each practice period, but vary our workout plans so that the practices will be as interesting as possible. However, we always try to utilize the basics that have been found to produce excellent results in match play.

5 THE LOB

THE LOB

By

Paul Assaiante

The lob is one of the more interesting strokes in tennis. Very few people respect its use, and yet these very same people are often incapable of countering it when it is used against them. Rarely will you hear a person say that a certain player uses the lob beautifully; yet the person who does lob well will be a very tough opponent. The lob obviously should not be a dominant aspect of a person's game but it can certainly be used as a means of intimidation against an opponent's attack. The lob can and should be used to keep your opponent from the net, to fatigue him, to exploit a weak overhead or poor mobility, to break his rhythm, to use the wind and sun as variables against him, and to totally destroy his confidence.

The lob should resemble the groundstroke. The only real differences should be in the racket face, which will be open, and in the follow through which will be much more vertical. Make very sure that you stroke the ball on the lob as opposed to pushing it or shoveling it. Both of these undesirable mechanics will result in short, feeble lobs.

The underspin lob is the best type of lob to use when you are on the defensive. The underspin gives you more control while it slows the ball down, thereby giving it a longer "hang time" in the air. On a windy day I prefer for my players to "hit out with underspin" with lobs into the wind. The reason for this is that the wind will help keep the ball in the court. Lobbing with the wind requires much greater feel, and I tend to discourage high lobs when the wind is to your back.

Many high level players train themselves to lob to their opponents backhand side. This is an excellent tactic which requires much control. I prefer for the average player, however, to lob cross court, since this will give him more court to work with and decrease his chance for error.

The offensive lob is usually hit with topspin. This occurs when the player decides that he can win the point outright by using the lob. This is a tricky lob to hit, however, and many people lose control by trying to use too much overspin. I prefer to execute this stroke as a high, rolling, softly hit groundstroke.

The reason most people lob ineffectively is lack of practice. Since one rarely uses the lob in a match, it is often neglected in practice. Do not make the same error as the average player. Never leave a practice session without at least spending some time on the lob and overhead, and while you do this you can watch yourself move up the club ladder.

1

2

3

4

5

6

Photos #1-3 illustrate how to properly hit a backhand lob. The stroke should resemble a ground stroke in every way except that the racket motion should be more vertical. The wrist must be firm in order to prevent weak lobs. The player should be careful not to look up too soon to see where the lob went if he wants to maintain control of the shot. Photos #4-6 show how to execute an offensive lob. Note that the stroke looks almost exactly like a forehand ground stroke. Only the follow-through gives this shot "away" and this disguise generally causes the opponent to react too late to properly react to this shot. Don't be overly cute. Simply step in and stroke the ball with the proper mechanics.

HOW TO SHARPEN YOUR TOUCH

**The lob, the drop shot and the half volley—
they're more than just croutons.**

By

**Barry Meadow
Contributing Editor, Tennis Magazine**

Some people think the touch shots of tennis are like croutons on a salad—nice, but not entirely necessary.

But if you never lob, terrifying sluggers will pitch a tent three feet from the net. Lack a drop shot and you won't get two-handed Floridians to come off the baseline. Have no half volley and notice how your serve-and-volley game becomes serve-and-error.

Some players don't practice these auxiliary shots because they know these strokes don't come up often in a match. It's possible to play three hard sets and hit six lobs, three drop shots and six half volleys. As a result, players neglect the touch shots and often can't produce them when they need them.

While many players take buckets of balls to practice serves, or bat endless forehands and backhands against walls, rarely do people practice touch shots. Perhaps this is the cause of the widespread but erroneous belief that only advanced players can use these strokes with confidence.

The lob, for instance, can be used by even the most humble of beginners. If your opponent is at the net, drive him back with a lob. Or float up a sky ball when you're drawn out of position and need time to recover. You can also use it offensively to win the point outright, particularly if you own a topspin lob.

To hit the lob, merely tilt your racket so the face is open as you meet the ball, and keep it open throughout the follow-through. A lob must be practiced on a court—walls are of no help because you can't tell how deep your

The Lob

lob has landed. Short lobs are about as useful as rubber checks.

If you don't have a practice partner, start by dropping a ball and lofting it, noting its depth. Then toss the ball several feet away to practice lobbing on the run.

If you have a practice partner, let him stand at the service line and feed balls to you. As you practice your lob from the baseline, he can practice his overhead. He should vary his feeds to you, so you can practice both forehand and backhand running lobs.

The lob is a valuable alternative to the passing shot. Throw up some lobs early in the match and your opponent won't be as likely to crowd the net. Then, as he hesitates, switch to passing shots.

The most common error in lobbing is failing to follow through. A short lob is a free point. It is better to lob too deep—at the least, to-and-fro chasing of your lobs may tire your opponent.

If you try an offensive lob, don't give it away by dropping your racket head. Take your normal backswing so your opponent won't know what's coming. Otherwise, your surprise lob will be no surprise.

Lobs are particularly effective on sunny days. Not only is it perfectly fair to lob into the sun, but you may intimidate your opponent into abandoning a net attack altogether.

Lobbing with the wind is easier than lobbing against it. Against the wind, a gust may convert that fine, deep lob into a sitter.

Use the drop shot with the lob. Draw your opponent to the net, then lob him. It's a perfect one-two punch against a baseliner on a hot day on a slow or non-skid court.

Just as a lob's major value can be psychological ("I hope he doesn't lob me, because my overhead's lousy"), a drop shot's chief function is to keep your opponent off-balance ("Will he hit a deep approach shot or try a drop shot?"). Use it to tire a slower or out-of-shape opponent by forcing him to run up for short balls, even if you give away a few points in the process. You can also employ it against an opponent's weak second serve to pressure him.

Hit a drop shot only when you're inside the court and your opponent is behind the baseline. At the beginning, use it only on balls that bounce within your service box. As you develop proficiency, you can try it on deeper balls.

When first learning the drop shot, hit it like a volley—no backswing and little follow-through. As you advance, deception becomes important. Take your regular backswing, but come underneath the ball to cushion it on your racket, and follow through in the direction you want the shot to go. This caressing action will cause the ball to die after it hits the ground on the other side.

Move in after your drop shot because your opponent will be forced to lift the ball. If you're close to the net, you can volley away his return. This also prevents him from answering your drop shot with another drop shot.

79

Note the high follow-through on the lob.

To practice the drop shot, stand just behind the service line as your partner feeds you balls. Try to hit this stroke so that it bounces at least twice within his service box. You can also have your partner stand behind the baseline and feed you short balls—you then mix deep approach shots and attempts for winners with drop shots. Play out these points so that your partner can tell you whether you're telegraphing your drop shot.

Don't try the drop shot from behind the baseline, or your opponent can reach it easily and knock off a winner himself. On some fast surfaces, drop shots are useless because they don't stay down. Don't skim the net with your drop shot, but allow a safety margin. While disguise is crucial to the success of a drop shot, don't resort to Julius Erving head fakes or you'll take your eyes off the ball and mis-hit the stroke.

The half volley is not a shot you'd like to hit, but one that you're forced into because you got stuck inside the court around the service line. You'll need to half-volley or short-hop the ball most frequently when following your serve to the net, but you may also stumble into one when you're playing doubles and are trying to get up, or in singles if you get caught in no-man's land. The half volley is the shot that can get you safely out of danger.

Be sure to bend for the half volley, rather than drop your racket head. Turn, and with a short backswing and firm wrist, lift the ball and follow through as you would on a groundstroke (the harder the ball is hit to you, the less of a finish you need). Always take this stroke in front of your body.

After you've finished the half volley, head for a position eight to 10 feet from the net. Then, unless your opponent hits a sensational dipping topspin that barely clears the net, that will be the last half volley you'll have to hit for that point.

Practice the half volley by standing at the service line and having your partner feed you balls to your feet. Hit the half volley, then follow it to the net and play the point to gain a realistic idea of the effectiveness of your half volley.

The major errors on this shot are failing to bend (resulting in a scooping action that presents your opponent with a ball he can clobber) and not finishing the shot (which gives him a short ball he can pounce on to pass you).

The lob, the drop shot, and the half volley—they're more than just croutons.

THE
6 OVERHEAD

THE OVERHEAD

By

Paul Assaiante

The overhead is often viewed as a nice shot to have, but as something not worth the effort to gain. As a result, many players never develop an adequate overhead and thus are hesitant about approaching the net.. Even if you have strong approach shots and solid volleys, you will always be exploited by an air attack of lobs directed towards your weak overhead.

The overhead is a tough shot to execute because you must time a vertically dropping ball which is often more difficult to gauge than a ball with a horizontal direction. In order to avoid getting fooled by a lob, I recommend using a motion which closely resembles the modified serve.

As you see the lob move off of your opponent's racket, you should get your racket up and into a "back scratch" position. Once you have accomplished this you can then forget your racket and concentrate on getting into a good position to strike the ball. Shuffle your feet so that you position yourself well behind where you would expect the ball to drop. This is important because most overhead errors occur as a result of letting the ball get behind you. Turn your shoulders and point towards the ball with your free hand. This will aid in your shoulder turn and in keeping the ball in front of your body. Then step forward while swinging up at the ball as you would hit a serve.

The ball should be hit a foot in front of the head and over the lead foot whenever possible. Everything about the hit of the overhead is similar to the flat serve: The racket gets up into a "back scratch position", the position of the body is sideways towards the net, the ball is hit a foot in front of the body, and the wrist snaps down on the ball for power. This big difference between the serve and overhead is in the angle of the racket face at impact. On the serve you try to utilize spin but on the overhead you usually try to hit a flat ball. The reason for this is two fold. Since you toss the ball on the serve, you can be assured of being able to pull the racket face across the ball. You do not have this assurance on the overhead. You are also able to hit the ball on a downwind trajectory because you are closer to the net on the overhead than on the serve.

You must spend many hours practicing your overhead if you wish to control the net. The biggest thing to remember is to stroke the ball aggressively on the overhead. I would rather hit a ball into the net or wide of the court than to shovel the ball back into the court. Hitting out and missing is simply an error, but the latter indicates a lack of confidence which will permeate the rest of your game.

1   2   3

4   5   6

Photos #1-6 illustrate how to execute the overhead stroke. Note that I point and turn my shoulders early in the stroke. This enables me "time" the ball which is dropping. I then take short, quick steps in order to get behind the flight of the dropping ball. This enables me to shift my weight forward into the ball at contact, which in turn provides more sting to my stroke. I would prefer to see my racket move to the backscratch position earlier than is shown in the above photo. Note that my actions in photos #4-6 closely resemble the modified serve (as they should). Remember to adjust your point of aim into your opponent's court by your position relative to the net. The closer you are to the net, the more offensive the nature of your shot. The further you are from the net at contact, the deeper should be your aim.

Photos #7-11 illustrate how to hit the backhand smash. Players should stroke this shot down the line because in the event that they do not put the ball away, they are in a better position to respond to their opponent's return. A crosscourt backhand smash is dangerous because the player is out of position to cover a volley if his smash is not a winner.

BE OVERLY PREPARED

By

David Benjamin
Princeton University

While watching a pair of club players flail at each other in a challenge match, you start thinking after a while that they're quite good. They're both hitting terrific backhand passing shots and many of the serves are clean aces. But suddenly one of the players is confronted with an easy lob. He tries to bury the set-up in his opponent's backcourt, but instead, mis-hits it and plops it into the net. Abruptly the club player doesn't look so good anymore.

It's a common story—the overhead is the acid test for distinguishing between a good club player and the experienced tournament player who looks upon a lob as an opportunity to hit an overhead and to gain an almost sure point. The club player views a lob with fear and loathing and prays that it goes out—anything to avoid hitting an overhead.

The good player will make 90 percent of his overheads. The average player will be pleased with 30 percent. In addition, missing an overhead is a psychological setback for the average player who was thinking "set-up."

The overhead is derived from the serve and should not be learned until you have mastered the basics of the service motion. Ideally, you should also have some experience volleying at the net, since that is the position where you will see the most lobs.

Theoretically, the overhead is a serve without a backswing. It is your answer to an opponent's attempt to lob the ball over your head. If he doesn't succeed, you'll have an opportunity to hit an overhead.

Assuming you are at the net and you've suddenly realized that your opponent's lob is a failure, get in the overhead ready position—turn your body sideways to the net, cock your racket behind your head (racket shaft parallel to your shoulders), point at the ball with your free hand, index finger extended, as if your finger were a direction finder. This spotting device enables you to concentrate on the flight of the ball and to keep the ball in front of you.

The Overhead

Most overhead errors occur when the ball gets behind you. But if you are able to keep the ball in sight with your forward hand until the moment of impact, there is no way you can make this mistake. Your feet will know when to back-pedal and when to stop because your pointer will help you determine how deep in the court the ball will go and when it will begin its final descent.

Your stance when hitting the overhead is similar to the serve, although slightly more open. All of your weight at impact should be on your front foot (i.e. left foot for a righthander, right foot for a lefthander). You should be on your toes for maximum leverage. Although many players jump as they hit a smash, it is safer to keep the front foot on the ground, especially while learning.

The point of impact should be roughly the same as that of the flat serve — comfortably in front of you with your racket fully extended. The shot is called an overhead for a precise reason and it should not be hit at shoulder or head height. So don't let the ball drop too low. This is where your ball-spotting index finger is an excellent aid — you will know where the ball is and when to begin your striking motion.

Once your racket head has made contact with the ball, continue your swing as in the flat serve, until your racket has followed through across your body and to your side. The momentum of your swing and all your body weight behind it should force you to bring your back foot forward. The forward motion of your back foot helps you maintain your balance and prepare you to move in any direction for a follow-up shot.

Once you have mastered the technique, the next question is tactics: where should you place the ball? Most players never even raise the question and this is their biggest mistake. They just bang away, becoming panic-stricken when their opponent returns their best smash.

The power with which you hit your overhead is no more important than the placement of the shot. In singles you should always try to hit your overhead deep into your opponent's court (the rear third of the court) or into the corner of the court farthest from him. In all cases leave a generous margin of several feet from the sidelines.

It is usually safer to hit your overhead crosscourt, since it will allow more margin for error. A bad lob which just hovers over the net can be put away by hitting straight down on the ball and placing it over the fence on one bounce. This tactic would be one of the rare times in singles that you would intentionally aim a smash in the shallow forecourt.

In doubles, an excellent tactic is to hit your overhead to either side of the opposing net man. Another prime target area is down the middle, a tactic that is good in almost all doubles situations.

Two other variations of the overhead involve the forecourt or midcourt — angle overheads. One (hit by a righthander) is hit with severe slice and slides away from your opponent. The perfect time to hit this is when you are

The Overhead

waiting for your opponent's lob on the extreme right side of your court and your opponent is standing directly opposite you on the extreme left side of his court.

The other angle overhead is the reverse smash. Instead of hitting straight down on the ball at the moment of impact, turn our wrist to the outside (away from your body). If you are right-handed, this motion will place the ball in the extreme right-hand corner of the service box. As in the slice overhead, the reverse smash relies on position and surprise and should be used with discretion.

There are also occasions when you should let the ball bounce before hitting it. If the lob is extremely high (over 30 feet), it is almost impossible to time to hit it on the fly. If the lob is high and close to the net, it is safer and easier to let the ball bounce, make note of your opponent's position and then put it away. If the lob is deep and high and lands close to the baseline, let the ball bounce and then hit it solidly as either an overhead or a groundstroke. Place it deep and set yourself up in good court position for the return.

The weather also affects how you play an overhead. A windy day will make an average lob seem like a knuckle-ball, and a sunny day can make an overhead a tearful experience. In both cases it's smart percentage tennis to let both lobs bounce and then place your return.

The final factor to take into account is spin. If your opponent hits a flat lob, no problem. If it's a lob hit with slice, it won't travel as deep as you expect. And if it's hit with topspin, watch out. Topspin causes the ball to fall faster than a normal lob, resulting in overheads hit too late or too low. If you see the topspin coming, start your swing a fraction sooner and hit the ball less forcefully, opting for control over power.

The only way to master the overhead, or any stroke, is with constant practice. If you are by yourself and have a backboard, you can practice endlessly by bouncing your smashes into the wall. If you're alone on a court, set yourself up by hitting a bounce lob in front of you and then smashing it. It is not the ideal way to practice, but it's better than nothing.

You can take turns with a partner with one player at net and the other in the backcourt. The backcourt player hits various types of lobs while the netman tries to smash them back to him. This drill improves timing, control and depth. Play for points with the netman trying to put the ball away and the backcourt player trying to lob skillfully enough to win the point. After a certain number of points, the players change position.

Another variation is the two-on-one drill. Two players are in the backcourt and lob the netman until he drops.

Doing overhead drills is important not only for timing, placement and control, but it also builds up stamina. A correctly hit overhead is the most tiring shot in tennis and the more tired you get, the easier it is to miss one. The more brutal the drill, the more likely that you'll have extra strength left for the last, and probably most important, smash of the match.

THE
7 APPROACH
SHOT

IT IS ALL IN YOUR APPROACH TO THE GAME

By

Paul Assaiante

In tennis tdoay with its greater emphasis upon offensive weaponry, a person must have a well balanced game just to survive the first round! One must develop sound groundstrokes, forcing approach shots, and put away volleys in order to be effective on all surfaces. To do this, the player must understand the differences between the three court zones, the strokes used in each zone, and when to move from one zone to the other. It is these concepts which will be explored in this article.

ZONE ONE — THE NEUTRAL ZONE

This is the zone from which play starts and where most of a player's time is spent during a match. It is located between the baseline and an imaginary line ten feet behind the baseline. It is the area where the serve is put into play, where the return of serve is executed, and where most rallying occurs. The reason I call this the neutral zone is because there is very little that you can do offensively from this position. You are thirty-nine feet from the net and seventy-eight feet from your opponent's baseline. Since you are far removed from these two areas, you are incapable of hitting many wide angled shots for winners. The most that you can hope for when you are in zone one is to move the ball around enough to force a weak return which would enable you to move into zone two.

ZONE TWO — THE ATTACKING ZONE

This zone is located between the baseline and just inside of the service line. It is the area that most coaches either avoid discussing or simply dismiss as "no man's land." I know of no way, however, for a player to get from the neutral zone (zone one) to the put away zone (zone three) without first passing through zone two. This zone is, in my opinion, the key to attacking tennis. The movement and the strokes used within it deserve serious consideration. The beauty of this part of the court is that the player never needs to venture into it unless he is following up a forcing serve or moving in on a weak shot. One word of caution, however, zone two is a transportation zone, in other words a zone through which one moves to get to zone three. If a person finds himself stuck in this zone after he has hit the ball, he is in serious trouble.

ZONE THREE — THE PUT AWAY ZONE

In this zone, the person should go for the outright winner. The closeness to the net allows for greater angled shots, and it is imperative that the player in this zone think extremely offensively for he may not get a second chance to win the point. What we see when a person is at the net is the visible final product. The put-away volley or the picture perfect overhead smash. Most people, however, do not realize that if the player had not executed properly in zones one and two, and had not moved through them at the proper time, he would not have had a chance for the winning shot.

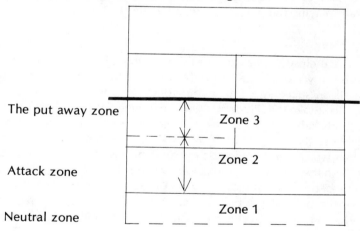

The put away zone — Zone 3

Attack zone — Zone 2

Neutral zone — Zone 1

THE TYPE OF STROKE AND THE MECHANICS OF EACH AS DICTATED BY THE ZONE

Zone One

In zone one, your goal is to move the ball around, and, most importantly, to keep it deep in your opponent's court. You should concentrate on taking a full preparation to insure more racket speed through the ball, and a full follow through to give you greater control over the shot. The long stroke is possible to execute from zone one because you are such a great distance from your opponent. From the neutral zone, you should utilize a topspin stroke which is accomplished by moving your racket from low to high in relation to the ball. Net clearance from this zone should be approximately eight feet in order to insure greater depth.

Zone Two

In the attack zone, your goal should be to stroke the ball deep into your opponent's court and then to move out of the zone and into a good volleying position. Do not linger in zone two because you give to your opponent a greater variety of shots which can be used against you. The preparation for this stroke should be fairly short because the ball will reach you sooner than normal. This is because you are closer to the net and it will take less time for a ball to reach you than it would take a ball moving at the same speed to reach you at the baseline. Your follow through should be a comfortably full one which will give you a greater degree of control over the ball. A word of caution about your footwork on this stroke should be mentioned here. You must move to and through the ball smoothly on the approach shot so that you are playing the ball rather than having the ball play you.

Zone Three

You are close to the net in this zone and, as a result, your preparation must be very short. Since you will have very little time to react to an oncoming ball on successive shots, your follow through must also be short. Attempt to step in the direction of the oncoming ball while cradling the racket with both hands. I like to see my players prepare their racket as early as possible so that the strings of the racket are placed in front of the flight of the ball well before contact is made. Picturing the racket as a magnifying glass with the subject (the ball) directly in front of the glass seems to help the players better understand this concept. Be careful not to move the racket out of the path of the ball during contact. Just move the racket forward slightly while letting a slightly opened racket face impart underspin on the volley.

MOVEMENT THROUGH THE ZONES

In zone tennis, the depth and speed of the oncoming ball determines when and how you move through the zones. The particular zone you have moved into should then dicate the type of stroke you should use. The simplicity of this concept is astounding but the development and use of it for each player is much more difficult. Keeping this concept in mind, watch a player at any level and you will be amazed at how often he or she violates the rules of movement or stroke production in each zone.

In zone tennis, the depth and speed of the oncoming ball determines when and how a player moves through the zone.

To better learn these concepts and how to utilize them yourself, try this progression. Go out to the local court and stand in each of the three zones. Bounce the ball and attempt to utilize the proper mechanical stroke as dictated by the zone. Then attempt to do the same with a ball that has been fed to you by a partner or by a ball machine. Once you feel comfortable with this last step, try to hit the proper strokes and to move into the proper zones while rallying with a partner. This step must almost be mastered before you can attempt to do the same things during competitive play. If you rush this last progression, you can be sure that frustration will ensue.

PRESSURE: THE WINNING APPROACH

By

Fred Stolle
Professional Editor, Tennis Magazine

If you are ready to move up to the advanced level, then you must already possess solid ground strokes, a good serve and a reliable volley. But having a well-stocked arsenal is just the beginning. Knowing what to do with it is another matter altogether.

Build your advanced game on the theme, "Take the initiative," which means attack. If you are the server, you can attack by following your serve to the net. But if you are the receiver, there is only one way to attack and that's through the approach shot. The approach shot is the gateway to the net and you must pass through it to get there.

PLAY THE PERCENTAGES

Why should you take the initiative and attack? Isn't the main style of play today centered around the baseline and long ground-stroke rallies? Yes, that is true, but if you watch the pros more closely, you'll see that those long points are usually concluded with one player at the net and the other trying to pass him. Baseline rallies are for thrusting and parrying, but to go for the kill, you most often go to the net.

As we discussed last month, Jack Kramer was a firm believer in percentage tennis—play the shots which pay off more often than not. He also believed in putting his opponent under as much pressure as possible. The place he did it was the net. If you rush the net, you force your opponent's hand. He must come up with a passing shot or a lob to avoid an almost sure winner. Since he must hit that shot from an unfavorable position, a position obtained by scrambling after your approach shot, it will be a go-for-broke attempt—one that will be a spectacular winner or a sure loser. Thus, the

Note the exaggerated topspin hit on this approach shot.

percentages are suddenly on your side when you rush the net. It is a simple, but frequently overlooked principle. Even if you do occasionally get passed, weigh your net rushes against your winners and your opponent's passing shots. I'm sure you'll end up ahead. If you don't, you should examine how you're hitting your approach shots and determine whether they are forcing enough.

THE MODERN APPROACH SHOT

The approach shot has undergone a change in the last 10 years. Ten years ago the world's dominant surfaces were grass and hard courts. Back then your approach shots didn't have to be too accurate, just deep in the court and aimed at your opponent's weaker stroke. Rallies were short. You just quickly hit an approach shot and rushed the net.

Today's tennis balls, however, are softer and the court surfaces are slower, with the dominant surfaces being clay and slow synthetics. Therefore you don't have as much margin for error. Your approach shots now have to be hit harder, deeper and more accurately. With the slower courts and balls your opponent has more time to set up and hit the ball. So, when you finally have an opportunity to rush the net, your approach shot had better be good or you'll be a sitting duck. That's why rallies are so long. Everyone has very strong ground strokes and passing shots, and the opportunities to attack are fewer.

An opportunity to attack does arise, though, when your opponent hits you a short ball. By short I mean the ball bounces inside or near the service line. Do not be over-anxious when you move in to hit the ball. Whether you are rallying or hitting an approach, don't beat yourself, don't rush. Take your time in preparation. Get your body going forward in the direction of your target. Some players want to get to the net at any cost. But if you're reaching the advanced stage and you are able to analyze the situation and sum up your opponent, find out what his weakness is during play and exploit it through the approach shot.

Never hit your approach shot off a ball between the service line and the baseline. Move in and hit the ball there and then quickly retreat to the baseline. Here discretion is definitely the better part of valor and smart strategy as well.

The approach shot is almost always hit with underspin, rarely with topspin. A sliced ball travels through the air more slowly than a topped ball and stays low when it bounces. The only time you might hit with topspin is when the ball is a sitter.

When should you hit an approach shot? There are a number of instances: on the return of serve, on critical points as a surprise attack. Rushing the net behind a return of serve is sometimes referred to as "chip-and-run." It is a good tactic on fast courts especially. Other surfaces well-suited to it are courts in high altitudes such as the courts in Johannesburg, site of the South African Open, where the ball travels through the air much faster than at sea level.

You shouldn't try the chip-and-run on your opponent's first serve, but on the second, particularly on important points such as 15-30 or 30-40 late in a match. Winning the point there would either give you two break points or the game. You should use the chip-and-run sparingly on other points to break up the pattern of your attack and occasionally use it early in a match when no particular pattern has been established.

The crucial points at any time of a match are when you have a chance to break serve or to gain a couple of break points. Your opponent is already under pressure because of the situation. By hitting an approach shot or a chip-and-run you will make him feel the pressure even more. If the server is down, 4-5, it makes even more sense to worsen his dilemma by rushing the net.

A surprise attack is another useful tactic with the approach shot. If the renowned baseliner Harold Solomon suddenly moved in on a short ball and rushed the net, it certainly would be a surprise to his opponent. And that shock might just be enough to prevent his temporarily flustered opponent from hitting a good passing shot.

The playing styles of the players at the top vary greatly. For example, Roscoe Tanner attacks more than Brian Gottfried. Why? Because he feels his game is built around his serve and volley. Gottfried has a strong all-around game and can stay in the backcourt with confidence. Borg will stay in the backcourt and so will Jimmy Connors and Guillermo Vilas, because they feel they've got the ground strokes. However, they all will attack and pressure their opponents in critical situations. Otherwise, they will find themselves in the position where they will have to come up with the big shot.

PLACING THE APPROACH SHOT

Anybody who has an all-around game is going to attack, because that's where matches are won. However, Solomon and Eddie Dibbs are counterpunchers and like people to attack them. They want a target to aim at, such as the lines. Borg is probably the master counterpuncher, but it is difficult to have to come up with the spectacular, low-percentage shot all the time. He is one of the few who can.

As I mentioned earlier, because of this new breed of players such as Solomon and Borg, your approach shots have to be accurate and forcing. Most times you should aim at the corners. However, you also may want to hit the ball down the center of the court to keep your opponent from getting an angle for a passing shot.

The most often used pattern on the approach is to hit the shot down the line and go to the net. Once at the net with your opponent hooked wide, cover his passing attempt by moving one-quarter the distance to the side he's hitting from. This coverage (also known as over-playing) will allow you to intercept any shots going down the line and crosscourt. If your opponent can hit the severe crosscourt angle required to pass you, congratulate him because he has hit a fine shot and has beaten the percentages. Should his passing attempt come near you, you can volley a winner crosscourt into the open-court area.

Sometimes you can play the percentages and still end up a loser. Gottfried got blasted by Vilas, 6-0, 6-3, 6-0, in last year's French Open final even though Gottfried attacked without a letup for three consecutive sets. He must have decided before the match that he would have to attack. He knew how well Vilas can control the flow from the back of the court. He wanted to pressure him out of his game, but the strategy didn't hold up. The same thought often goes through the minds of the Australian players when they play Ken Rosewall. Ken has such superb ground strokes, especially his backhand, that opponents never would play him from the backcourt.

The first step in developing an advanced game is learning how to pressure your opponent from the net position, having earned your way there through a forcing approach shot—the second step is learning how to reply to this pressure yourself, when an opponent seeks the net position. The modern power ground stroke—as demonstrated by Guillermo Vilas and Jimmy Connors—is how you fight back when you're the one being pressured. Next month our study of the advanced game will cover how to be aggressive with your ground strokes.

The first step in developing an advanced game is learning how to pressure your opponent from the net position, having earned your way there through a forcing approach shot—the second step is learning how to reply to this pressure yourself, when an opponent seeks the net position.

THE APPROACH SHOT IN TENNIS

By

Dean A. Austin
University of Wisconsin, Green Bay

The approach shot is probably one of the most neglected skills in tennis. By definition, this shot is a half-court offensive stroke which allows the player who executes it to assume a position at the net. This maneuver makes it possible for a baseline rally to end in a point-winning volley. A good approach shot gives one player the advantage in a match between individuals of equal strength.

When a player is locked in a baseline rally, there are two ways he can win the point: 1) He may continue rallying the ball deep on the opponent's court, hoping that his opponent will eventually hit the ball out-of-bounds or into the net; 2) He may take the offensive by gaining the net position to score the point-winning volley. The latter method utilizes the approach shot. This shot's strength is that it permits a player to gain a net position—the area where winning tennis is played. Although the approach is a relatively simple shot, it is seldom practiced and is often utilized improperly.

Perhaps one reason for the neglect is that many players and coaches do not make a distinction between the approach shot and the baseline drive. Basically, the approach shot is an offensive attacking stroke, while the baseline drive is a defensive stroke. For this reason, there are several differences in the way the shots are executed. Some of the differences are racquet preparation, stance, contact point, aiming point, position on the court, and follow-through. The description and Illustrations 1, 2, 3, and 4 are based on the forehand approach shot; however, they are also applicable to the approach shot.

Racquet preparation (backswing) for the approach shot is somewhat higher and shorter than it is for the baseline drive because the ball is to be directed straight over the net with a little topsin in order to bring it down on the opponent's court. The player's feet should be in an open stance about shoulder-width apart with the front foot (left foot if the player is right-handed) dropped back approximately 6 inches and turned toward the net. His trunk should also be turned about 50° toward the net. This position enables the player to use deception in executing the shot which prevents his opponent from determining where the ball will be placed and what type of shot will be hit.

As the racquet is brought toward the ball, the player's hips should be tilted forward slightly. This hip angle, combined with the high backswing, allows him to hit the ball with a flat trajectory. At the same time, he prepares the racquet to sweep over the back and top of the ball. At the same time, he prepares the racquet to sweep over the back and top of the ball. The sweep provides the topspin that is needed to bring the ball down onto the court sooner and shortens the flight of the ball. The racquet face should be closed slightly as it approaches the ball and the racquet's movement should be parallel to the court surface. It is important that the racquet remain level throughout the stroke. The follow-through ends in front of the player's body with the racquet face almost perpendicular to the court surface, still closed slightly, and pointed toward the net.

If the ball a player intends to hit as an approach shot falls below his waist, a variation in the execution of the shot is necessary. Again the racquet is prepared short and high, but in this instance, it should be positioned slightly to the outside as well. Thus the racquet can be wiped across the ball from the outside in rather than sweeping over the back and top of the ball. The player's main concern should be to return the ball just over the top of the net. He does this to force the opponent to return the same kind of shot. Now, however, the player who is using the approach shot will be at the net ready to volley the return for a winner. This net position gives the player an opportunity to hit down on succeeding shots because he is on the offensive and, therefore, in a far better position to win the point.

In addition to execution, another basic difference between the approach shot and the baseline drive is the aiming point. The baseline drive is aimed high—3 to 5 feet over the net and deep on the opponent's court; however, the approach shot is aimed no more than a foot over the net and is placed about 2 feet behind the opponent's service line near one of the sidelines, preferably the opponent's backhand sideline. This placement forces the opponent to stay well back on his court and prevents him from making a powerful return. It also opens the court for the return volley. With the opponent pinned near one of the sidelines, the net man is in an excellent position to end the rally with a well-placed volley.

Following is a brief summary of the important steps in executing the approach shot:

1) The normal baseline drive stance is opened by dropping the front foot back about 6 inches.

2) During the backswing, the racquet should be positioned higher and shorter than it is for the baseline drive.

3) While the forward path of the racquet is parallel to the court surface,

the racquet face is closed slightly and is wiped over the back and top of the ball to apply topspin.

4) The player's hips should be tilted forward as the racquet approaches the ball.

5) The ball should be aimed at a point a foot over the top of the net and about 2 feet past the opponent's service line near one of the sidelines.

If a young tennis player is to learn the forehand and backhand approach shots properly, he must be provided with good instruction and the opportunity to perform the shot often.

Here is a progression which can be used in teaching or learning the approach shot:

1) Describe and demonstrate the various segments of the stroke.

2) Have the players execute the stroke slowly as each movement is outlined.

3) Without using a ball, have the players execute the stroke over and over until it is done properly.

4) At this point, the novice is ready to use the ball. First, have him toss the ball to himself. Then have a partner toss the ball to him slowly and with a bounce that is at least waist high.

5) Incorporate this same progression in learning the backhand approach shot.

Once these basic drills have been mastered, the coach can divide his team into pairs, placing each player at a baseline. One of the players can set up the approach shot situation by hitting his baseline drive short which places it near the service line. This gives his partner an opportunity to move well inside the baseline, execute the approach shot, and position himself at the net for the next shot. After the approach has been made, the baseline player should hit the ball at the incoming net man. If the net player does not place his volley for a winner, then the point is played out.

Finally, the players may simply rally from the baseline. When a baseline drive falls short, the player moves inside the baseline to execute the approach shot and the point is played out. Once again, the coach may stipulate that the return after the approach shot must be aimed at the incoming net man. Then the point is played out.

Teaching the approach shot will lead naturally to the concept of net play and its importance in winning tennis. A coach should emphasize the importance of the approach shot to his players and stress the concept that winning tennis is played at the net. A player should realize that in order to win the net from the baseline, he must be able to gain the net on his serve or have an approach shot which will enable him to move to the net. If both players have equal ability at the net and the baseline, the player who has a good approach shot will certainly have the advantage.

8 DOUBLES PLAY

WATCHWORDS FOR DOUBLES

By
Bob Bayliss,
US Naval Academy

Perhaps the biggest key to the success of the Naval Academy tennis program in recent years has been our attention to doubles. There are a few areas in which the intelligent player can score heavily. In a nutshell they are:

1) **Play the Percentages.** Don't hit shots you do not usually make. The dimensions of the court and position of your opponents dictate the necessary shots. Don't defy these two factors. Flat shots are generally not as desirable as those with topspin or underspin. When out of position, drop back and lob.

2) **Return Service Consistently.** Leave the bullet returns of serve to Connors and Laver. If you are not consistent with a topped return, make sure you chip the ball. Move in a little closer for the second serve. If you are playing against an opponent with an especially big first delivery you can't handle, bring your partner back with you and throw up some lobs. This tactic is also helpful if you find yourself constantly out-volleyed in rallies at the net. On a particularly weak serve, both you and your partner should close in to get you into the net quickly. This puts a lot of pressure on the opponent's first volley.

3) **Play the Middle.** When in doubt, a low ball down the middle is the safest shot to hit in most instances. Move in behind your shot and cover the middle yourself. By doing this you force your opponent to hit a well angled (and more difficult) shot to win the point.

4) **Get Your First Serve In.** You have the deck stacked in your favor when you are serving. Don't blow this opportunity by serving a lot of second balls and allowing your opponent to gamble and hit an offensive return.

5) **Don't Be Afraid to Poach.** On at least an occasional basis, be sure to cross. Even if you lose the point, you may win the next one because the receiver will be watching you instead of the ball. When you do poach, do so by angling toward the net, rather than parallel to it as you move. When you encouter a strong cross court return—especially in the backhand court—try the Australian (tandem) formation. You can poach off this too.

6) **Don't Let Deep Lobs Bounce.** Take them in the air, even if you have a weak overhead. By letting them bounce, you give up that sacred net position and, for all intents and purposes, the point.

7) **Move In, Move In. Move In.** It's so easy to retreat in the face of fire. The only great teams have been those which dominate the net. Be aggressive.

STRATEGY IN SERVING DOUBLES

By

Dr. R.H. Williams
State University College, Cortland, New York

Many of our college players who had played competitive high school and/ or junior college tennis believed that their main purpose in serving doubles was to get the first ball in and take the net as soon as possible. Where the serve landed was not considered too important.

Any tennis coach would agree that the first serve in doubles should go in, at least most of the time, and the server should get to the net as soon as possible. However, it is our belief that strategy begins with the serve. Thus, the net man, as well as the server, should know where each serve is to be placed so that the receiver's angle of return is reduced.

To reduce the angle of return, our doubles teams used only two areas of the service courts. Diagram 1 shows these two areas in each service court. The areas labeled 1 were called center and those numbered 2 were called outside.

If the net man had no knowledge as to where his partner intended to serve or if his partner served to the outside area most often, he had to remain close enough to the alley to prevent the down the alley return by the receiver (Diagram 2A or Diagram 2D). However, this position gave the receiver more court to use in returning the serve to the server, if and when the serve landed in the other areas of the service court.

The center court theory was an agreement between partners that the net man would position himself as far from the alley as practical, approximately 4 to 5 feet away from the alley and 5 to 6 feet away from the net (Diagram 2B or Diagam 2C). The center area was the primary target for serves, and unless communication between the partners indicated a switch, the net man knew the serve would be to that area. Communication was by signs, silent or vocal, and with practice these signs were easily exchanged between partners, even between the first and second serves.

The serve was considered the best offensive shot and the server was expected to hit the designated area. However, each server had a pet serve and usually one area of the service court was easier to hit than the other. Thus, he, rather than the net man, determined when to switch to the outside area. Also, he had the right to reject his partner's signs, even the common poach (i.e., the net man cutting off the receiver's return to the server). However, if he accepted the sign, he had to serve to a predetermined area and be prepared to cover the opposite half of the court.

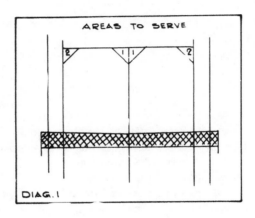

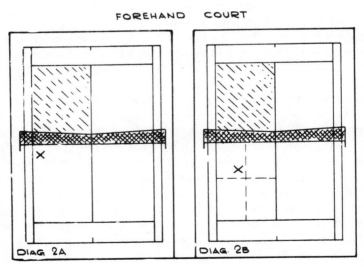

BACKHAND COURT

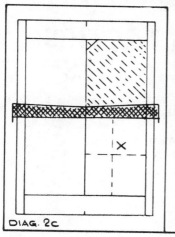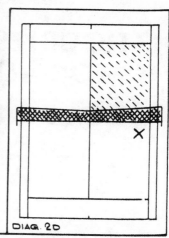

DIAG. 2C   DIAG. 2D

Often, this position by the net man was an invitation or perhaps it should be called a temptation for the receiver to hit to the net man's alley, or return a defensive lob. Either return was to the advantage of the service team, because the defensive lob had to be placed deep and near the baseline or an overhead usually ended the point. The down the line return, especially when the serve was to the outside area, seemed unguarded. However, the net man had prior knowledge of this serve and if he felt too far away from the alley, he moved to his outside while the service ball was in flight. Otherwise, he maintained his position and concentrated on not allowing the return to get by the alley side. When the serve was to the center area, whether the attempted return was to the server or the net man's alley, the playable court was reduced by this position.

The main purpose of the center court theory was to cut down the receiver's angle of return and make him attempt returns that were not to his advantage. In fact, whenever the receiver made a service return, other than to the server, we believed it was to our advantage.

It took considerable practice for our doubles teams to acquire confidence in the center court theory, especially the net men. However, the many receivers who tried time and time again for the short cross-court or the down the alley return, when the serves were to the center or outside areas respectively, made it easier for them to accept. Even when the returns were to the server, the possibility of the pick-off or poach by the net man was greater, especially the latter, since the net man had less distance to go to complete this cut-off tactic.

Give center court theory a try. Even though the angle is shorter and the net higher, many receivers will try for the alley rather than the return to the server.

DOUBLES TACTICS FOR ALL LEVELS

By

Chet Murphy
University of California, Berkeley

In our article, "School and College Doubles," which appeared in the March issue, we discussed certain tactics suitable for either advanced or middle-class school play. It will be noticed that many of the moves and formations can be used interchangeably at all levels of play. Teachers and coaches have the option of deciding which tactics are appropriate for their players. Here, as in the matter of form on strokes, there is not only one best way to play for all levels. What works is best, and what works at one level may not work at another. Experienced coaches are quick to adjust the tactics and strategy of their teams; they select whichever style of play is compatible with the capabilities of their players and the quality of the competition. However, while doing so they do not ignore basic principles of position play and movement—principles which make even special variations more effective. Some of these have been discussed. This discussion of doubles play will be continued by listing several additional principles that should be considered when teaching, regardless of the level of play.

THE OFF-CENTER POSITION

In doubles, as in singles, experienced players move to be in position to bisect the angle of returns when an opponent is hitting from a sideline or alley. They move in order to be slightly off-center, either to the left or the right of the center line, depending on whether they are at the net or in the backcourt.

PLAYING AT THE NET

When they are in the volley position, partners must move left or right, up or back, depending on the position of the opponents and the type of shots

110

When an opponent is hitting from an alley in doubles, the opposing net man should move in that same direction to protect his alley (Diagram 1). Diagram 2 shows the net man turning to watch his partner hit from behind him, thus deriving an early indication of his partner's intentions. An alternative method is shown in Diagram 3. Here the net man is looking toward his opponents to key on the opposing net man. In either case, Diagram 4, when the opponent diagonally opposite from him has a play on the ball, the net man moves toward the center to protect the opening. Diagram 5 shows the baseliners properly off-center when the opponent smashes from the sideline. In Diagram 6, the smasher hits deep to the opponent's backhand so that the smasher's partner can poach and intercept the return.

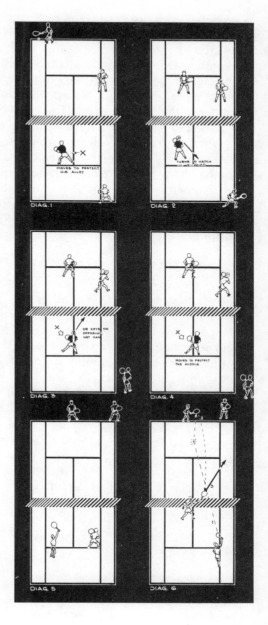

111

expected from them. When an opponent is hitting from close to the center mark, the primary concern of the partners should be to protect the center of their court. Most of the opponents' shots will be aimed there; therefore, it is important that this area be well covered.

However, when an opponent is hitting from close to a sideline, both net men should shift toward the sideline sufficiently to protect against both a shot into the alley and one toward the center. The man closest to the sideline protects the alley; his partner protects the middle.

When an opponent is hitting from a short, wide angle, the net man must cover both a shot along the line and a sharply angled cross-court shot. To do so, the player farther from the hitter must move up and toward the center line to intercept or at least discourage the angle shot, while his partner must move to protect the alley. We find it necessary to remind our players constantly to protect against a sharply angled return when they have hit one to their opponents.

PLAYING FROM THE BACKCOURT

When playing from the backcourt, the players must work as a team to protect the center of their court and to protect against wideangled returns from the opponents. Making the opponents hit from the center, whether they are at the net or in the backcourt, reduces the angles for their returns and often lures them into hitting to the center. Protecting the center then is an easy matter, partners move toward the middle and let the stronger player make most of the plays.

Occasionally, however, a baseliner's shot must be angled sharply. An example would be when he is keeping the ball away from an opposing net man. Consequently, an opponent will be hitting from over close to a sideline. When this occurs, both backcourt players must move to protect against a wide-angled shot; they must be off-center away from the hitter.

This tactic is especially effective when an opponent is smashing a lob from close to a sideline. Smart defensive players move away from that sideline a bit to cover the area diagonally across the court from the smasher. This not only places them in a position to cover the smasher's strong shot, but also often tricks him into aiming to his smallest opening, thus developing an element of risk in his shot.

MOVING IN TO ATTACK

When backcourt lobbers intend to attack after a weak smash by an opponent, they may often be able to move in a step or so even before the smash is hit. This occurs when they have succeeded in catching an opponent off-balance and have him struggling to reach the ball as he goes back to hit. Moving up close to the baseline places them in a position to attack on a weak return. Here again, the hitter decides whether to move up or not and

112

his partner acts accordingly. If they move up and the approach shot forces an opponent wide to hit, the net men move to be off-center in that direction.

RETREATING TO DEFEND

If the smasher is getting set to hit aggressively, the baseliners should usually retreat to a point 12 to 15 feet behind the line to play defense. The farther back they go, the more time they will have to make a play on the ball, but they will also be required to cover a wider angle. Sometimes it may be best for them to stand in a compromise position halfway back, to reduce the angle offered to the smasher while at the same time providing sufficient time to move to reach his smash. Even then they should be off-center enough to protect against the wide-angled shot and a shot along the long diagonal dimension of the court.

RELATING POSITION, TRAJECTORY, AND SPEED

One of the most misunderstood and yet easy to teach principles of doubles play is that position and the height of the ball being played determine the proper trajectory and speed of the shot. Ideally, in a fast net exchange, players want to volley through an opening in their opponent's court, or to volley hard enough and quickly enough to cause them to miss. Often the opponent's positions and shots prevent that shot. In such a case, the intention should be to hit low to the feet of one of the opponents causing him to hit up. To do this, a player must gauge his speed and trajectory by considering his distance from the net and from the opponents, their position from the net, and the height at which he is stroking the ball. If he is hitting at a high ball he may be able to hit it hard and still place it low to their feet; he may be able to hit along a diagonal line straight to their feet. If, on the other hand, he is hitting at a low ball, he will have to hit it easily enough to permit gravity to bring it down after it clears the net. He must use a low trajectory.

Hitting a low trajectory from a low volley often requires that the player hit the ball back much easier than the speed at which it came to him. We say he must "take the speed off the ball." For this he loosens his grip at contact and drags the racket slowly across the ball, rather than punch at it as he does to hit crisp volleys.

TEAMWORK AT THE NET.

When at the net in an attacking position, a few simple rules agreed on beforehand will enable partners to play together smoothly. All balls hit straight along the center line should be handled by the player in the left court because his forehand is toward the center. When the opponents hit successive shots to the center within reach of both net men, the player who hit the last ball should take the next one. Most players establish a rhythm when they hit successively this way. Conversely, players who are left out of a rally for two or three shots often do not time their next shot properly because they are not able to follow the ball closely. This is especially true in a fast net exhcange but it often applies when the opponents are in midcourt or even near the baseline. An exception occurs, of course, if one player is markedly stronger than the other. In this case, the stronger player should make the play.

Rules to follow when opponents lob to our attacking net men are also set up. Naturally, all short lobs are hit aggressively in an attempt to win or to draw an error. Smashers are warned, however, not to aim to a small opening or a short angle if there is a larger hole or a longer angle. If the lob is too deep to be played aggressively the smasher should aim to the backhand of the weaker opponent, or to the feet of either opponent trapped in midcourt. On lobs between the two net men, the man with the strongest overhead should be allowed to make the play. And even on short lobs over to his partner's side, the strong player is expected to play all he can reach and handle, provided he calls out his intention in time to avoid confusion. He calls "mine" or "I have it" and moves in confidently to play, knowing that his partner is moving to get out of his way. Partners have agreed that a voice call is never rescinded, and that when each of them makes a call the first one made is in effect. They never ignore a call, and never overrule one call with another. To do so can often be disastrous.

Most high lobs are usually difficult to judge and time properly. For this reason our players are urged to let such lobs bounce and to make an overhead play after the bounce. Generally, a high lob is dropping vertically or nearly so and it usually bounces vertically or nearly so. Consequently, the smasher does not have to retreat an appreciable distance to make his play after the bounce. Here our smashers are encouraged to go for a winner if they have a safe angle or an opening. If not, they should aim deep to the backhand of the weaker opponent. The smasher's partner, knowing this, moves up to the net position to poach on the opponents' return after the smash. Usually, the weaker player is in the right court. The smash then, hit to his backhand, is hit to the center. This permits the poacher practically to ignore his alley regardless which side of the court he is on. He moves toward the center strap to intercept. If the smasher chooses to hit toward an alley, because he feels he has a good angle or an opening there, the poacher may have to stay in place to protect that alley.

When one of the net men is forced back to smash a deep lob, players often become confused and fail to act as a team. Many times the player making the smash returns to the net position only to discover that his partner has retreated. At other times, the smasher retreats while his partner mistakenly waits at the net, assuming the smasher will return to join him. Plainly, neither is a desirable situation.

Note how in doubles play, a player must get into the net by following his/her own serve.

In order to prevent such misunderstandings, we set up the following rules: The man who is making the smash decides whether his team should retreat to the backcourt or return to the net position after his hit. His partner should watch him as he hits for an indication of what he intends to do and then must act accordingly. He either retreats to the baseline with the smasher and takes up a defensive position, or he stays at the net, knowing his partner will join him there. We feel this procedure is logical because the hitter knows best how well he can hit his smash. His intentions as he smashes should be determined, in large measure, by his position and depth in the court. If he feels he has been forced back too deep to be able to return to the volley position, or if he feels the lob is too good to permit him to smash aggressively, he retreats and calls his partner back with him. If, on the other hand, he feels confident about making a good smash, he returns to the net position. The smasher's partner can often anticipate his moves and his intentions by noticing his position as he smashes.

Smart net men move to be in good position for all shots including lobs. When they anticipate a lob, they back away from the net a bit intending in that way to be able to reach the ball and smash aggressively. Inevitably, the opponents surprise a net man and succeed in lobbing completely over him. This occurs often in strong-and-weak doubles, where the weaker player stands exceptionally close to the net to compensate for lack of volleying ability. If this occurs when a net man's partner is in the backcourt, the backcourt player simply crosses over to make the play. His partner, meanwhile, crosses over to the other side so that together, they have both halves of the court covered.

If both players are at the net and a lob clears one of them, then retrieving is a more difficult matter. Normally, the man to whose side the ball is hit is responsible for all balls in his direction. If he has moved too closely to the net, which is probably why the lob got over him, his partner may be in a better position to make the retrieve even though his run diagonally across the court is longer than his partner's run parallel to the sidelines. We find this is the most effective way for inexperienced players to make the retrieve. Most of them are better able to play the bounced lob when running sideways and half facing the net than when they are in full retreat with their backs turned, completely to the net. Here, also, the net players simply exchange sides. The net player either moves over to be in position to volley from the side left vacant by the backcourt player, or retreats to the baseline to play defense. This should be determined by the type of shot the retriever is making. If he can protect his partner with a low shot to the opponents' feet the team may choose to play from the one-up, one-back position. If the retriever is in trouble, it may be necessary to give up the net position.

POACHING

In top-level doubles play, net men often poach to intercept returns at the net. Poaching at that level of play is used both offensively and defensively.

For offense the net man moves across the center line to intercept a shot that would normally be his partner's. He poaches because he is in better position, he can use his stronger stroke due to the fact that he has a better angle on his shot. For defense the net man moves to cover openings in his court caused by his partner being out of position.

The art of poaching lies in being deceptive. A good poacher conceals his intentions, sometimes by "playing possum" and standing perfectly still before making his move; other times by constantly shifting, swaying, and shuffling in place to confuse the opponent. In the first instance, the poacher often surprises the hitter by sneaking across to intercept a normally good return. In the second, he often distracts the opponent and causes a hit to be missed. Sometimes he lures the opponent into hitting straight at him as he holds his ground after making a fake or two.

Poaching is used most frequently on the return of serve. Sometimes it is a spur-of-the-moment decision by the net man. Other times it is planned beforehand and the server serves accurately to make it effective. He aims to the center of the opponents' court to make it possible for his partner to leave his alley vacant without too much danger of being passed there. On a wide server, the net man has to hold his position to protect the alley. However, most top teams have signals to indicate the net man's intentions. Probably the most frequently used signals are a closed fist and an open palm. The server's partner, for example, places his left hand behind his back to show the server a closed fist. This signifies that he intends to sneak across the center line to intercept the return. The server, therefore, starts up to the net in the normal manner but changes direction after a step or two and dashes over to protect the side of the court left vacant by the poacher. In contrast, the open hand signal means the net man intends to hold his starting position. He usually fakes a poach to confuse the receiver. When using this plan, the server stands close to the mark so he can reach a good volley position in the other half of the court if it becomes necessary.

Top-level teams poach during rallies as well as on return-of-serves. The technique, here, is similar; the poacher waits until the last split-second, until the hitter has committed himself, then moves across to intercept. These moves are often preceded by fake moves intending to rattle and confuse the opponent. At times the fakes lure him into hitting directly to the net man who holds his ground after a fake.

In top-level play poaching is often carried out successfully from the so-called Australian formation described previously, in which the server's partner stands on the same side of the center line as the server. From that position he moves across to intercept returns, either by an instantaneous decision or according to plan and with signals with his partner. Usually, this formation is used to take away a receiver's effective cross-court returns; it forces him to return down the line. Occasionally, it is used to combat effective net play by the receiver's partner, who may be good at poaching on the server's first volley. In this unconventional formation, the server's first volley is being played from the opposite side of the center line from the opposing poacher. From there the volley can easily be kept out of his reach and placed to the receiver.

Although our discussion of poaching has dealt mainly with its use in advanced play, intermediates and beginners can learn to poach effectively. They, too, can increase the range of their reach by making frequent, well-timed moves to the center line. At this level of play, what we call stepping out is emphasized, rather than the wilder, all-or-none dash across the line seen so often in advanced play.

The net man simply skips sideways, toward the center, as the opponent makes his hit. From this new position close to the center line he can reach across the line with a cross-over step to intercept a return, or can reach back toward his alley to protect his half of the court. As players develop skill, they seem to expand their reach naturally so that soon they are moving clear across the line in one continuous dash. The one big drawback to poaching at this level of play is that the server cannot always place his serve down the center line. If the serve is wide, of course, the net man must hold his position to protect his alley. But even the stepping out can be done effectively if players learn to return to their starting position when the receiver aims there. Indeed, stepping out, when combined with the fakes and feints described previously can trick the receiver into hitting to a waiting net man even at this level of play.

DRILLS FOR WINNING DOUBLES

By

Harold G. Wall
Woodside, California, High School

Each tennis season we rely on the doubles teams to win the greater part of our matches. For this reason considerable time is spent working on strategy and using drills that encompass the skills which they use in competition. In almost all of the drills, we have the players work from the positions they play during a match such as forehand or backhand court. In this way, they gain confidence in playing that position, and the coach can work on doubles strategy with both partners or one at a time.

Through these drills each player improves not only his tennis skills, but

118

at the same time learns how much court he can cover, what position he must be in to enable him to use a particular shot, and where to return shots in his opponent's court.

The practice schedule for our doubles teams usually follows this pattern: After general team conditioning drills, the first and second doubles teams go to the two end courts. There they are given three minutes of reaction drills. Then they practice their groundstrokes from the baseline for ten minutes. For the next 45 to 60 minutes they will use the drills which accompany this article. The players may spend more time on one drill than on another depending on their strengths and weaknesses. After the drills, both doubles teams will play each other, and during this time we will interrupt frequently to explain strategy or to correct strokes.

Over the years, we have been fortunate in having boys who enjoy playing the game of doubles and who work hard on the drills to perfect their skills. Our players take pride in being a member of a doubles team because they know they are important to the total success of the entire team and do not have to take a back seat to the more publicized singles players, which is so often the case.

Following are the drills which we use to train our doubles teams.

1. REACTION DRILL. A. The coach or a manager leads the drill by pointing in the direction he wants the players to move. Point to right, player A moves to the right and simulates a volley, and player B moves over to cover the middle.

B. Point to left, player B moves to the left and simulates a volley, and player A moves over to cover the middle (Diagram 1). C. Point back for a lob, both players A and B go back for a lob.

2. STROKE-DEVELOPING DRILLS. A. Net shots. Both players A and B take their normal net positions. The coach or a junior varsity player takes a basket of balls and starts to drop and hit balls at medium speed alternately to each player. Both players practice placing shots at short corners and down the middle. The coach can place empty tennis ball cans where he wants the players to hit balls. Stress that the players stay on their toes and keep their rackets up and ready (Diagram 2).

B. Return of the lob drill. The players take net position, and then the coach or a junior varsity player hits high, deep lobs. Both players go back for the lob and either return the ball with a lob or a smash. This drill enables the coach to emphasize that both players should go back together and shot. As soon as they have made the return, they should both go back to net positions.

C. Approach shot, first volley, and put-away. Partner A takes his baseline position, his partner B has a basket of balls and is stationed on the other side of the net. Player B will hit a ball to A who should hit a good approach shot. Player B will hit a second ball at volley height to the service line where A will hit his first volley. Then B hits a third ball so that A who has reached net position can put it away. Player A then goes to the backhand court and starts over again. They switch every five to six minutes. During this drill we emphasize hitting a deep approach shot, stopping, setting for each volley, and most important, moving quickly and with good control (Diagram 3).

D. Serves and service return. Each player A practices his serves trying for control and not speed. Every other serve should be placed in the backhand corner using a twist serve. Player B work on their return of serve trying to hit the three basic types of returns: one, the return that would land at the approaching server's feet: two, down the alley return, and last, a lob return. After the server serves 20 to each side, they change places (Diagram 4).

E. Fast volley, Player A takes his net position, and player B positions himself on the opposite side with a basket of balls. He drops and hits balls to player A as fast as possible. Player A will try to volley each shot with good control. This drill helps the player execute fast exchanges at the net by developing his reflexes and concentration on hitting a ball and readying himself for the next one.

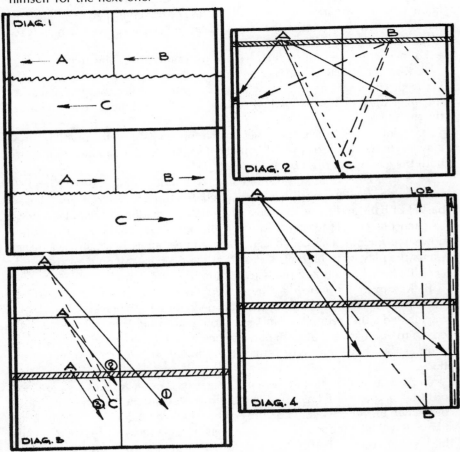

F. Overhead smash. Player A takes his position at the net. Player B or a junior varsity player hits or throws short, high lobs. Player A hits overheads, trying to place his shots at the short corners and down the middle. Players who are working this drill should try and hit each shot with maximum power because this is the put-away shot and they must develop confidence in it.

When working these drills, the coach or a manager instead of hitting balls can throw them. Often, throwing the balls results in better control, and time is saved because each ball is placed where the coach wants it to go.

EFFECTIVE PRACTICE SESSION FOR NET PLAY IN DOUBLES

By

Charles Tobey
Brooklyn College of the City University of New York

Doubles is an important part of every team tennis match, and in close matches the ability of these players will often determine the final outcome. It is important that once the doubles teams are selected, they be given practice in the skills that will make them an effective team. Merely playing a considerable amount of doubles may not help, because players simply continue to practice their poor techniques and increase their bad habits.

One of the keys to success in doubles is to be able to gain an offensive position at the net, maintain it, and have the opponents playing from a defensive back court position. Good doubles teams seek every opportunity to come to the net so that they can aggressively and authoritatively force the other team to yield their positions. For doubles players to be able to assume this kind of commanding position at the net, they must work diligently and hard at their net games and overheads.

Some drills that can be used in a single practice session or as segments of several practices sessions are:

1. Have the doubles team stand side by side and close to the center line where they can easily get in each other's way. As they are fed low hard shots over the net, they will have to learn to work together as a team and adjust to each other's strengths and weaknesses.

2. Break the volley into two parts, forehand and backhand, and work each individually for 10 minutes. Thus the player will not be allowed compensate for his own weakest stroke by moving around it.

3. Have each doubles team hit overheads for 10 minutes.

4. The situation where all four players are in front of the service line and trying to win a point is not that rare in doubles but is seldom practiced. Bring both teams up to net and have them volley competitively against each other. This is done by having the players volley the ball over the net to each other three times, and on the fourth the ball is in play as each team tries to score the point.

5. In order to develop the ability and the desire of both players to rush the net in a set of doubles, play regular doubles using a 50 point scoring system. Each man serves 5 times in succession and whoever scores 50 points first wins. Points are scored in the following manner: a. One point if the point is won with one or both players in back of the service line when the opponents hit the ball. b. Two points if a point is won with both players in front of the service line when the opponents hit the ball.

6. Play a match, emphasizing the need to be aggressive and maintain offensive positions at the net.

If a team spends a great deal of time practicing doubles and learns to work together effectively, the players will have an advantage over other teams that spend little time working on this segment of the game. Since team matches that are decided in the doubles (not clinched in the singles) are necessarily close, they are often between fairly evenly matched teams. With skills of individuals being nearly equal, such intangibles as having developed the ability to play the net offensively, as a team in doubles, might be the deciding factor in determining team victory.

SCHOOL AND COLLEGE DOUBLES

By

Chet Murphy
University of California

Although aggressive net play is essential for successful top-level play, it is not always possible nor is it always the winning way in school and college doubles. At these levels players often lack many of the qualities and skills needed for a constantly attacking style of play. Many youngsters, for example, cannot serve or volley well enough to move in safely on every serve. Most high school players and average college players also have the same limitations. And among average club players, whether men or women, teenagers or veterans, these deficiencies are even more apparent. This does not mean these players cannot win in doubles at their level of play.

When teamed properly with a partner who has compensating skills and when they devise tactics that permit them to make the best use of each other's abilities, they can, indeed, play effectively. In this discussion of doubles, we will describe several variations from conventional advanced formations, variations that often permit a weak server, a slow mover or even a poor volleyer to enjoy doubles and to win a good percentage of the time when playing within his class. The idea is that he and his partner devise tactics that permit them to play within their capabilities, regardless how these tactics differ from those of top-flight, all-around players.

The One-Up, One-Back Formation The most obvious variation we recommend from top-flight doubles is in total plan of play—the strategy. Rather than attempting to win by moving in to the volley position immediately, a team may often be more successful using the one-up, one-back formation. They can use the special individual qualities and talents of each player while at the same time avoid having to use many of their weak strokes and shots. The intention with this formation is to allow the good driver to play from the backcourt (to use his drives) while the good volleyer plays from the net (to use his volleys).

The Backcourt Player. If one player of a doubles team dislikes being at the net and does not play well there but can rally steadily and accurately from the backcourt, this then, the backcourt, should be his base of operations. After serving, he remains at the baseline to play with his strength. He also stays back after his return-of-serve. He moves in to the volley position only when drawn in by a short shot or when he feels an attacking drive of his is strong enough to do so safely. Since accuracy usually develops along with steadiness, a good baseliner can usually manage to keep his drives out of the net man's reach. When the opponents make a very good attack shot, he may have to lob. Most good baseliners are good lobbers because this ability seems to develop along with steadiness and accuracy from the backcourt. Consequently, he may find that lobbing even the return of serve is an effective tactic at this level of play.

When teaching this formation, we emphasize that the baseliner's chief function is to protect his partner who is at the net. He protects his partner in several ways depending on the position of the opponents: 1) If they are also in the one-up, one-back formation, he drives deep to the other baseliner; 2) if both of the opponents are at the net, he drives low to the man farther back (if they are equidistant from the net, he drives low over the center strap or to the weaker player); 3) if the opponents have made a very good attack shot, he lobs, sometimes on the return of serve, other times during a rally. His direction for each lob is determined by several factors. He aims either to (a) the weaker player, (b) the poorest mover, (c) the shortest player or (d) the player caught off-balance or out of position. Sometimes he even chooses to disregard all these factors and lobs cross-court to minimize the chances of lobbing short. He selects the long diagonal dimension of the court which provides a greater margin of safety than does a lob parallel to the sideline.

These same shots that are used to protect a net man often draw weak returns that he, the net man, can put away for winners. In a sense, a baseliner plays to protect his partner, while also trying to set him up for a kill. The net man is in an attacking position but at the same time he is in a position to be attacked. It is imperative, therefore, that the baseliner hit either deep or short, (depending on the circumstances) to keep him out of trouble.

The baseliner's second function is to advance to the net on the first safe opportunity, unless, of course, he feels hopelessly inadequate there. For this the requirements are the same as designated for the singles approach shot. When he is hitting his strong stroke from inside the baseline, he is in a position to attack safely. He aims either deep to the opposing baseliner or directly at the opposing net man to draw an error or another weak shot. We urge him to *pick on* the net man when the opponent is caught so close to the play that he cannot defend himself. If our own baseliner is fearful of ever being at the net, he stays in the backcourt to use his ground strokes to set his partner up for a winner.

Frequent use of the lob is emphasized in our doubles instruction, especially in middle class play. In our opinion, the overhead smash is the weakest shot among players in this class. The logical shot, therefore, for getting out of even the least bit of trouble against opposing net men, is a lob. Especially when one of the opponents poaches effectively, we emphasize lobbing over him. We say, *The more he bothers you, the more you must play at him, with drives down his alley and lobs over him.* Even if the lob does not draw an error on his smash or does not get clear over him, it may still restrict his poaching moves a bit and so leave more room for cross-court drives.

We have already suggested that lobs should be aimed at the player with the weaker overhead. At times, however, the man with the strongest overhead may be so far out of position that the safest lob is to his half of the court. This decision, whether to lob to him at all, must usually be made on the court after the pattern of play has been established. Frequently, however, a coach or a team may decide which of these plans to follow before play begins, basing their decision on what they already know about the opponents.

Lobbing the return of serve is one of the most effective plays in doubles of this class, especially when done from the right court. Coincidentally, this is usually the side on which the weaker receiver is stationed and the opposing

Chipped returns of the serve are an important aspect of doubles play.

net man is eager to poach. The receiver, unable to control his drives or slices well enough, may have to resort to the lob as his most frequent return, as a defensive play if for no other reason. A lob that clears the net man on his half of the court completely disrupts the attacking team. But even more effective in the long run are lobs to the other half of the court, to the baseliner. The purpose is to keep the ball as far away from the poacher as possible. Frequent use of this play tempts net men to attempt to reach many balls that they are not able to play effectively. They often become impatient waiting for a setup and roam out of their territory. When this occurs, they soon begin missing more smashes than they make. Then, as their team falls behind in the score, they try even harder to dominate play and thereby compound the fault. This is a common occurrence in school doubles where a strong player is often paired with a very weak player.

The Net Man. When playing in this one-up, one-back formation, the net man may sometimes play only three or four feet away from the net. If his partner can always hit deep and accurately, or low when necessary, this close-in position may be the most effective way to play. Often, however, the opponents' attack shots place a baseliner in trouble, in which case his net man should prepare to defend himself, because the opponents are likely to close in and attack him. For this purpose, the most effective position for the net man is usually 8 to 10 feet away from the net.

Regardless of his starting position, the net man must be constantly on the move during the point. He should move toward his alley when an opponent is hitting from that alley, and toward the center to intercept when an opponent is hitting from the center. When he senses the opponents are in trouble (one of them is forced back deep to hit, or is hitting at a half-volley from midcourt), he should move up to play aggressively, and he should move back to defend himself when they are closing in on him. He may even have to retreat to the baseline to play defense when his partner lobs.

When his partner is forced wide into the alley, the net man should move in that direction, to close up the hole left between them. He moves to give the opponents two small holes to which to hit, one on each side of him, either of which he can cover better than the larger opening developed by the opponent's wide shot. This means he must turn to watch his partner whenever he is hitting from behind him. He should watch only long enough to notice his partner's court position and to anticipate his intentions. Then he should look toward the opponents, ahead of the ball, to defend against the possibility of the opposing net man intercepting the return. The important thing here is that the volleyer should always be alert to move—to move forward, backward or to either side—for the purpose of defending his half of the court and covering any holes left by his partner's moves. By turning to watch his partner, he gets an earlier indication of his responsibilities than if he watches only the opponents. At times, however, the net man's partner may be hitting from up so short in the forecourt that it is impossible to watch him hit and also look ahead of the ball to the opponents. In this case, the net man has no choice but to direct his attention to the other net man and respond to his moves.

The Server. In school competition in which the one-up, one-back formation is used, the server is not always able to serve well enough to attack. Instead he is content merely to put the ball in play. Even with this plan, however, the server should aim to the receiver's weak stroke, which is usually the backhand. To do this consistently, the server must serve from the proper location. There is some difference of opinion among teachers and coaches regarding the best place from which to serve. Our experience has led up to conclude that the following procedures are usually effective.

When serving from the right court, the server should stand close to the center mark. This gives him a straight-down-the-line shot to the receiver's backhand and places him in good position to handle returns with his forehand (we are assuming, always, that at this level of play the backhand is the weaker ground stroke). If he has trouble placing the serve to the backhand from that centered position, however, he should stand over close to the sideline. Then the receiver, placing himself properly to bisect the angles of the serve, will be exposing more of the court on his backhand side than he did on serves from the center. The server need only move a step or two to his left after having served to protect his own backhand from the receiver's return. Coincidentally, when serving from this position, the server is provided with a convenient target at which to aim. He should try to hit the triangle he sees out beyond the net, formed by the center service line, center strap, and the service line. Occasionally, however, the server aims wide to the forehand to prevent the receiver from covering his backhand completely. If the receiver is not properly bisecting the angle of the serve, and is covering his backhand too much, frequent wide serves to his backhand are often effective.

When serving from the left court, the most effective location from which to hit to the receiver's backhand is close to the alley. From there the server has a diagonal shot to the backhand corner, while at the same time he is in a position to cover his own backhand. Only when the receiver lobs well enough to clear the net man, or when he is a left-hander, should the server stand close to the center mark. Then he may even hit from a compromise position, halfway between his alley and the mark.

Even at this level of play it is important that the server put a good percentage of first serves in play, even if they are hit at only medium speed. He must avoid having to serve a *cream puff* second ball and must somehow keep the server from moving in confidently on every serve. An occasional hard serve is necessary, therefore, to keep the receiver guessing. And here, depth of the serve is important. We urge our net men to keep the server informed about the placement of the serve and especially about its depth. Usually the server is too busy moving into position to notice whether his serve is short or deep. A word from the net man who is always in position to notice can be a big factor in improving the serving team's chances.

A variation of this serving formation can often be used effectively when the server is unable to avoid having to play returns on his (or her) backhand. This is often seen in mixed doubles play when the lady serves from the left court but it works well in boys' and men's school play.

To prevent the left court receiver (who is usually the stronger player) from driving to his backhand, the server stands close to the mark to serve. His partner, meanwhile, stations himself on the same side of the center line, at the net, and faces the receiver. Here the purpose is to force the receiver to return along the right sideline. The receiver hits away from the net man, to the baseliner's forehand. The server moves over quickly after having served to be in position to play the return with a forehand. Then the rally continues with him in a good position to play only forehands. Balls aimed to his backhand are likely to be within reach of the net man who can play them with his strong forehand volley (Illustration 1).

Still another variation of the one-up, one-back formation can be used to take advantage of the respective strong points of the games of doubles players. The stronger player of a team dashes to the net on every one of his serves and on his returns. Meanwhile, his partner starts in the backcourt and remains there throughout the point. When serving from the right court, the strong player should stand close to the center mark and run forward and to his left to volley. His partner stands at the baseline, to the right of him, and remains there throughout the point. From that location he is able to use his stronger forehand on almost all balls hit to his half of the court. When serving from the left court, the strong player runs straight in to volley while his partner again stays in the backcourt to play from there. This is a rather unusual arrangement but it often works. We coached a high school team in boys' competition to win a state championship with these tactics. The weaker player never approached the net. He stayed in the backcourt and played defensively, protecting his partner and setting him for *kills*. His partner, meanwhile, roamed all over the front court and intercepted everything within reach.

Choosing Sides. One of the first problems coaches and players face when forming doubles combinations is deciding which player is to play from the left court and which from the right. When one player is much weaker than the other, the logical place to put him is in the right court. There are two reasons for this: 1) he is less likely to have to return the serve with his backhand because it is more difficult for most servers to place the ball there than when serving to the left court; and 2) after the serve is in play, most balls aimed to his backhand can be played by his partner with his forehand.

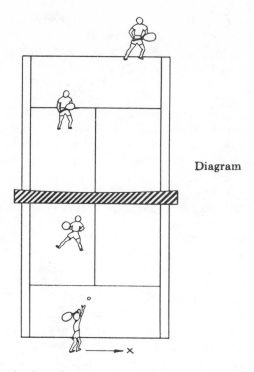

Diagram

This is true whether the team is at the net or in the backcourt. In the backcourt, there is almost always time for the left court player to sneak over and take more than his share of balls hit to the center. But even at the net, the stronger player can often react quickly enough to protect his partner's backhand. And, most important, this formation is effective against lobs, because the strong player can manage to play a forehand smash on most lobs, even those aimed to his partner's half of the court.

There is also another plan that sometimes works to protect the weaker player, one that may be used when he can volley at least reasonably well with his forehand. To permit him to play with only that stroke, he is placed at the net on the left side, closer to the sideline and closer to the net than a regular net man should be. From there he makes a play only on those balls he can reach comfortably with a forehand volley. He leaves so little room on his backhand side, his alley, that the opponents do not risk hitting at such a small target. And from his close-in position, practically on top of the net, he is no longer a weak volleyer. Consequently, the opponents soon learn to keep the ball away from him. This, of course, is the reason for using this for- mation; the stronger player covers more than his share of the court, plays more than his share of the shots, and hits deeply enough to protect his net man. This requires a great deal of agility and stamina on his part but in competition where winning is more important than playing politely, this is often the effective way. We recommend these tactics for middle class school play.

Playing Parallel. In top-flight doubles, players start in the one-up, one-back formation. One player of each team starts in the volley position, and his teammate moves up to join him on both the serve and return of serve. We have suggested continued use of the one-up, one-back formation in middle class school play. A third strategic plan is known as playing parallel. It is used a great deal in school play, and more often than occasionally in top-level play, when the receiving team feels they cannot return the serve well enough to attack on their returns. It works equally well whether the opponents play together at the net or play in the one-up, one-back formation.

A description of this formation is implied in the name itself — playing parallel. Partners are always equidistant from the net (or nearly so); a line drawn from one of them to the other would be parallel to the net. This is true whether they are playing from the backcourt or from the volley position. If they decide to change locations during a point and move from the backcourt to the front court, they do so together, thus staying parallel. Normally, the parallel formation in the backcourt is used only by the receiving team. It can often be used effectively by the serving team in low-level play, however, when they cannot serve well enough to move in and volley the return of serve. Admittedly, this is not the way doubles should be played, but it may sometimes be the best way, considering the equipment and abilities of the players involved.

Mixing Defense with Attack. When the opponents move up to volley together, the team playing parallel at the baseline usually has a twofold plan: They play from the backcourt, hoping to draw errors with a mixture of drives, slices, and lobs. In addition, they advance to the net together when given the opportunity on a short shot from the opponents. When the opponents are in the one-up, one-back formation, the backcourt team plans their attack differently. They rally deep, keeping the ball away from the opposing net man, while waiting for a short shot from the opposing baseliner. When it comes, they move in together to attack, hitting deep to the baseliner, or, when hitting from very close in, directly at the net man or into his alley. They advance to the volley position after their drives hoping to finish the point with volleys or smashes.

At this point a few words of warning may be appropriate to teachers and coaches who are not familiar with this style of play. It is not unusual to see inexperienced players become confused about tactics when playing this plan. Often the hitter strokes and remains in the backcourt, feeling he is not able to make an effective approach shot, while his partner moves in to attack. This, of course, takes them out of the parallel formation and puts them in the untenable position of playing half offense and half defense in the one-up, one-back formation behind a weak approach shot. Unless their defense is good, they present their opponents with an opening between them behind the net man.

To prevent this from happening among our players, we set up a definite rule to guide a team's action. The player making the play on the ball decides whether his team is to attack (and move up to volley) or to continue to rally from the backcourt. His partner watches him closely while he hits, looking for an indication of his intentions and then acts accordingly. If the hitter decides to stay back, his partner stays back with him. If the hitter moves up as he hits, his partner moves up with him because presumably the hitter feels he is able to make an attack shot.

Parallel for Defense. The parallel formation can also be used for strict defensive doubles—the type of play that wins so often in low-level school play where neither partner can volley well. We encourage some of our young teams to play this way until they reach a point in their development when they can attack. We encourage them to think of patrolling the baseline, and try to instill an attitude of *they shall not pass.*

To play good defense, good lobbing is essential. Our feeling is that players at this level develop lobbing skill more quickly than they do skill at hitting overhead smashes. And since for every one of our lobs the opponents are required to hit a smash, we feel our players are more likely to be using a relatively safer shot than are the opponents. Lobs are not aimed in an indiscriminate manner; however, each one is aimed in a definite direction for a specific purpose. If one of the opponents is caught up too close to the net, the lob goes in his direction. If one player is shorter than the other, he is easier to lob over. But if one is obviously weaker at smashing, he gets most of the play. A slightly more sophisticated plan is to lob continually to the player most likely to crack under pressure.

Besides having these choices when lobbing, defensive players may sometimes wisely choose to lob cross-court simply to have the long diagonal dimension of the court along which to hit. This can be especially effective when the lobber is hitting from the alley or from outside the lines. A lob crossing the net diagonally from there often causes confusion between the opponents. If often appears to them to be within reach of both. Indecision about which player is to make the play often leads to a weak play—sometimes an error, other times no play at all.

A final choice defensive lobbers may consider is a low lob to the backhand of the weaker opponent. This shot need not be a true lob; it may even be a soft high drive. Only ranking players can hit high backhands aggressively. A semi-defensive shot placed there will draw many errors among average players and should be used frequently as a change-up to low drives and high lobs.

9 CONDITIONING FOR TENNIS

CONDITIONING AND STRENGTH TRAINING FOR TENNIS

By

Paul Assaiante

There appears to be ever growing support by physiologists and coaches alike, regarding strength training as a supplementary program for the athlete. I have given this much consideration, and have found it to be a very effective and important part of the daily regimen of a tennis player.

First, we must divide tennis season into two phases. The first phase, or the "out of season" portion of our program, would encompass that time frame in which the player would not be involved in competitive matches. This could either be a pre-season or post-season drilling and training time. It is during this time frame that the tennis player should utilize a strength training program. The second phase, or the "in season" portion of our program, encompasses the competitive match time frame. During this time strength training should be avoided.

While "in season," the player is involved in match play and is devoting most of his practice time to the *mental* and, to a lesser extent, physical preparation. It is during this time that I have my players practice the various court drills to improve foot speed. These drills usually last five minutes a day and involve rapid movement to and fro within the court simulating match type pavement. We spend five minutes a day jumping rope which also helps in this area. During the "in season" part of the program, I also have my players take three long slow runs a week (in excess of three miles) in order to maintain a strong cardiovascular endurance base. The final daily conditioner involves abdominal exercises which I feel are essential for all tennis players year round.

As you may have noticed by now, the "in season" program does not involve any upper body strength work. Although upper body strength is important for tennis, the strength training involved to create it may actually adversely affect your performance. Different people react differently to the strength workout and some may find themselves stiff or sore for a day after the workout. A person with a match the next day cannot afford this. Thus, the weight lifting program should occur during the "out of season" program where this would not be such a traumatic experience.

During the "out of season" period, players should lift every other day so as to avoid overtaxing the muscle groups. Lifting every day will cause fatigue and ultimately injury. The weight lifting should involve light weights, a high number of repetitions, and a short recovery phase. The players should use a weight which can be lifted a minimum of 20 times within 45 seconds. The recovery time between stations should not be longer than 30 seconds.

The program should involve 8-10 different exercise stations which should tax as many different muscle groups as possible. The muscle groups that we concentrate on are:

Abdominals	Pectorals (chest)
Forearms	Latisimus Dorsi (back)
Deltoids (shoulders)	Quadriceps (thigh)
Triceps (upper arm, back)	Hamstrings
Biceps (upper arm, front)	Gastrocnemius (calves)

This program can be effectively organized while using free weights, Universal machine, or the Nautilus machines. At West Point we are fortunate to have all three and allow our players to select the equipment they would like to use.

Do not misinterpret my drift. We are not trying to create muscle men with bulging muscles. We are merely trying to improve upon the player's upper body strength so that all the strokes have more zip and sting to them. Lifting while following these brief guidelines will enable your players to improve upon their strength without risking physical injury.

Fit To Win:
How to Organize A
Muscular Fitness
Program for Tennis

By

James A. Peterson, PhD
Stanford University
and
Daniel P. Riley
Penn State University

Many muscular fitness programs are unfortunately based upon hand-me-down information—information that has been handed down over the years from the weight lifter, to the body builder, to the coach, and eventually to the athlete. The athlete in turn passes on this information to others and the cycle continues.

An athlete or coach should not rely on hand-me-down information to organize his muscular fitness program. Scientific principles, not someone's intuition, should be the only basis for organizing a program.

When organizing a program to develop muscular fitness, an athlete or a coach is confronted with seven basic variables on which the program should be based. Although there are many ways in which these variables can be manipulated to produce an increase in an athlete's level of muscular fitness, the recommendations presented in this chapter offer the athlete—in our opinion—the most effective and efficient approach for achieving maximum improvement.

The seven basic variables of a muscular fitness developmental program are:

1. What exercises should be performed?
2. In what order should the exercises be performed?
3. How many repetitions should be executed?
4. How much weight should be used during each exercise?
5. How many sets of each exercise should be performed?
6. How much rest should be taken between exercises?
7. How many workouts per week?

Exercises to be Performed

At least one exercise should be included for each major muscle in the body (the lower back and buttocks, the legs, the torso, the arms, and the abdominals). As a general rule, the total number of exercises for the major muscle groups should not exceed ten to eleven. An additional two or three exercises for muscles specific to tennis (e.g. hand muscles, forearm flexors, etc.) can be incorporated into the program to bring the total number of exercises in the program to fourteen.

The specific exercises to be performed will be dependent upon the equipment the athlete or coach has available. While some equipment is certainly better than other equipment, the most important factor for the athlete to remember is the fact that the key to improvement is not necessarily the tool but how he uses it. Table 1 presents a listing of the traditional strength training exercises for the various major muscles of the body.

Order of Exercise

Whenever possible, the athlete should exercise the potentially larger and stronger mucles of the body first. The athlete should progress from the muscles of the legs, to the torso, to the arms, to the abdominals, and finish with the muscles of the neck. The muscles of the neck are exercised last because of the fact that these muscles possess a relatively (in comparison to the rest of the body) low base level of fitness. It is simply imprudent, safety-wise, to continue strength training after the neck musculature is fatigued. The abdominals are exercised after the legs, torso, and arm muscle groups because for some exercises (e.g. the squat), the abdominals are a stabilizing factor. If the abdominals are fatigued before the legs, torso, and arms, when you perform an exercise involving the abdominals as a stabilizer, you either compromise the intensity at which the exercise can be performed or the safety level of the lifter. The arms are exercised after the torso because the arms assist in exercises involving the torso (e.g. bench press, military press, etc.). The same limitations—either a decrease in intensity potential or an increase in the possibility of an injury occurring—exist.

While exercising the muscles of the torso and the arms, the athlete should attempt to alternate pushing and pulling movements whenever possible. Although in many instances an individual could follow any order of exercises and improve his level of muscular fitness, he should remember that one of his major goals, whenever possible is make his conditioning program as efficient as possible. Do Not Sacrifice Efficiency!

When determining your order of exercises, you should group your exercises by their designated body part (legs, torso, arms, abdominals, neck) and alternate pushing and pulling movements for the torso and arm muscles.

Legs—buttocks, quadriceps, hamstrings, calves.
Torso—deltoids, lats, pectorals, lower back.
Arms—triceps, biceps, forearms.
Abdomen—obliques, rectus abdominis, transverse abdominis.
Neck—flexors, extensors, trapezius.

While exercising the muscles of the torso and the arms, the athlete should alternate pushing and pulling movements.

138

Exercise by Muscle Group and Equipment

	Free Weights	Multi Station Equipment	Variable Resistance Equipment
Buttocks/lower back	squat stiff-legged deadlift	leg press hyperextension	hip and back leg press
Quadriceps	squat	leg extension leg press	leg extension leg press
Hamstrings	squat	leg curl leg press	leg curl leg press
Calves	calf raise	toe press on leg press	calf raise on multi-exercise toe press on leg press
Latissimus dorsi	bent-over rowing bent-armed pullover stiff-armed pullover	chin-up pulldown on lat machine	pullover behind neck torso/arm chin-up on multi-exercise
Trapezius	shoulder shrug dumbbell shoulder shrug	shoulder shrug	neck and shoulder rowing torso
Deltoids	press, press behind neck upright rowing, forward raise side raise with dumbbells	seated press upright rowing	double shoulder 1. lateral raise 2. overhead press rowing torso
Pectoralis majors	bench press dumbbell flies	bench press parallel dip	double chest 1. arm cross 2. decline press parallel dip on multi-exercise
Biceps	standing curl	curl chin-up	compound curl biceps curl multi curl
Triceps	triceps extension with dumbbells	press down on lat machine	compcount triceps triceps extension multi triceps
Forearms	wrist curl	wrist curl	wrist curl on multi-exercise
Abdominals/obliques	sit-up side bend with dumbbells	sit-up leg raise	sit-up on multi-exercise leg raise on multi-exercise side bend on multi-exercise
Neck	neck bridge (dangerous)	neck harness	4-way neck rotary neck neck and shoulder

Table 1. Basic Exercises for Strength Training

How Many Repetitions?

The number of repetitions which each exercise should be performed is based upon the athlete's subjective evaluation of the validity of two schools of thought. The traditional philosophy recommends that the number of repetitions to be performed is dependent upon the goals of the program. If the athlete wants to develop strength, he should perform sets of 5 to 8 repetitions. If he desires to build muscular endurance, he should perform sets of 9-15 repetitions. The primary proponents of this philosophy are free weight enthusiasts and Universal Gym users.

A contrasting theory which has been developed in the last ten years is the philosophy which recommends that regardless of your personal muscular fitness developmental objectives, sets of 8-12 repetitions should be performed. The Nautilus Sports/Medical Industries equipment proponents are the major advocates of this approach.

Regardless of your personal philosophy regarding the relative merits of the two contrasting techniques, you should categorically reject the mentality that insinuates that "more is better." There is obviously a point of diminishing returns regarding the expenditure of effort. The goal of your conditioning program should be to develop fitness in an efficient and effective manner possible—not engage in lengthy workouts merely for the sake of working out.

How Much Weight?

The athlete should initially learn how to properly perform each exercise before progressing to an effective weight. Once the correct techniques have been learned, the athlete, through trial and error, should select a weight that will cause him to reach the point of muscular failure somewhere between his arbitrarily predetermined number of repetitions. The point of muscular failure has been reached when the athlete can no longer raise the weight in good form through the muscles' full range of movement.

If the athlete fails before he reaches the minimal number of the predetermined lower limit of repetitions, the weight is too heavy. If he can properly perform more than upper limit of repetitions, the weight is too light and more weight should be added. The "overload principle" should be observed if the athlete is to increase his level of muscular fitness. The overload principle simply states that the athlete should, whenever possible within his personal limits and within the recommended guidelines for developing muscular fitness, to increase the amount of weight used or the number of repetitions performed during the execution of each exercise. Once the predetermined number of maximum repetitions are reached, the athlete should have a training partner assist him to perform two or three additional repetitions in order to achieve additional gains in strength and endurance.

Running should be an integral part of your conditioning efforts.

How Many Sets?

A set involves the number of repetitions executed each time an exercise is performed. Similar to the controversy surrounding the question of how many repetitions should be performed, two major approaches exist concerning the number of sets which should be performed. The traditional philosophy states that three sets should be performed. The contrasting theory recommends that only a single set be performed. The reasoning basis for this theory holds that one "properly performed" set will stimulate maximum gains in muscular strength and mass. If an athlete properly performs one set, he will certainly not want to perform a second set; and if he did perform additional exercise, it could eventually become counter-productive. If a second set is performed, it is obvious that the first set was not properly performed. Advocates of this philosophy argue that too many athletes associate gains in strength with the number of sets performed, totally disregarding that it is how each exercise is performed that stimulates strength gains. When multiple sets are performed, some athletes can be observed "holding back" and pacing themself for the last set to be executed. Although this method of training can produce significant gains, the time spent is prolonged and unnecessary.

Regardless of the philosophy which you adopt, one of your objectives should be to organize a workout that will produce the maximum level improvement in the most efficient amount of time. The two hour weight training workout is neither needed nor productive. A three-set workout typically requires only approximately 1 hour to complete, while a 1-set workout takes less than 45 minutes.

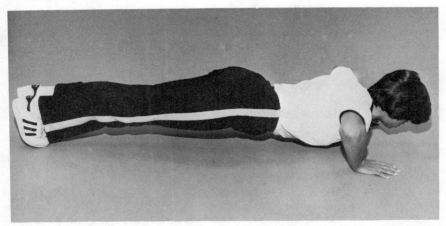

Regardless of your conditioning philosophy, one of your program objectives should be to organize a workout which will produce a maximum level of improvement in the most efficient amount of time.

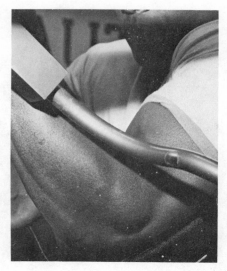

A muscle, when overloaded, needs at least 48 hours to fully recover.

How Much Rest Between Exercises?

In general, an athlete should move from one exercise to the next, allowing only a minimal time to rest between exercises. If you were to observe a "typical" strength training workout, you would find, in many instances, an athlete spending more time resting between exercises than he actually spends lifting weights. A reasonable rest period between exercises is somewhere between 30 seconds and 1 minute. Any greater rest period can lead to a time-consuming, prolonged training session. An athlete can develop his level of aerobic fitness, concurrently with his efforts to increase his level of muscular fitness, by moving from one exercise to the next in a non-stop fashion. This method of training consumes less time and places a substantial demand on his cardiovascular system. As a result, his level of aerobic fitness is improved.

How Many Workouts Per Week?

If a muscle is not exercised every 48-72 hours, it will begin to atrophy (grow weaker and smaller). Also, a muscle when overloaded, needs at least 48 hours to fully recover. During his off-season, an athlete should train three times per week on alternate days. During the in-season period, an athlete should work out at least twice, and preferably three times a week to maintain his muscular fitness level. The in-season workouts should include two high intensity workouts and one less vigorous workout. The less intense workout should be performed in between the two high intensity workouts.

A stronger athlete is a better athlete.

GUIDELINES FOR CONDUCTING A MUSCULAR FITNESS PROGRAM

Regardless of the equipment you use or the program you adopt, you must adhere to three basic guidelines if you want to achieve maximum results.

- Exercise through the full range of movement. If an athlete does not perform every exercise through the full range of movement, he eventually will lose flexibility in the particular joint area, as well as fail to develop muscular fitness through the full range of movement.
- Exercise antagonistic muscle groups. Within the body, there are four major antagonistic (opposing) muscle groups.

> Chest — Lats
> Biceps — Triceps
> Abdominals — Lower Back
> Quads — Hamstrings

When one muscle group (of a pair) contracts as the prime mover, the opposing muscle groups (of a pair) lengthens and vice versa. In order to reduce the possibility of injury, it is very important that an athlete exercise both muscle groups (of a pair). When one group of an antagonistic pair becomes disproportionately stronger, the likelihood that the weaker muscle group will suffer an injury (e.g. pull, sprain, tear, etc.) is increased.

- Emphasize the lowering of the weight as well as the raising of the weight. Many athletes when lifting will concentrate on raising a weight, but once in the mid-range position of an exercise, they'll "drop" the weight to return to the starting position for the exercise. Remember the same muscles which raised the weight are also the same muscles which will enable you to lower the weight. Don't circumvent *half* the exercise.
- The two most important principles for developing muscular fitness are supervision and intensity. Supervision involves doing every exercise properly — repetition after repetition. Intensity requires that the subject lift to a point of maximum muscular fatigue — the point at which the lifter cannot perform a proper repetition of the specific exercise in good form.

145

10 TENNIS TECHNIQUES

"WHEN IT'S TIME TO LEAVE THE CLUB"

By

Vic Braden
Tennis Professional

For every tennis player, good or bad, there comes a time when his or her position on the ladder must be assessed, and a decision made whether to move up or forever be sentenced to one rung. I will here talk about this crossroads as it applies to a fairly good club player thinking of moving into regional tournament play. But many of the essentials covered can at least to some degree be adapted by players of lesser experience, so don't be put off if everything that follows seems a bit beyond your skills. With sufficient practice—and, as we shall see, practice is the key—*everyone* can improve.

For top club players to broaden their horizons into regionals is really a jump into pre-professional play, and many professional disciplines will apply. Amateurs at this level lack only complete development of their strokes and proper mental preparation, but, unfortunately, they are apt to be arrested at this stage, because one of the barriers to further progress is that their evaluation of themselves is inaccurate. Very few people really know who they are as tennis players.

For instance, we recently had a nationally ranked junior, and we were talking about difficult shots; one was a cross-court passing shot from a base line corner of the singles court deep into the opposite service court corner. "I do that all the time," the junior said, "just ask my coach." I said I didn't have to ask his coach, I'd just get him out there and have him prove it. "And I'll let you bounce the ball," I offered, "and you don't have to hit it fast, and I'll bet you *still* can't do it with any consistency." So he bounced the ball and hit it, and the best he could do was about 40 percent on one side and about 25 percent on the other. It turned out he didn't own that shot at all.

Then, how *do* you find out who you are as a tennis player? You must learn how to chart yourself in match play. Or, rather, have someone chart your play for you; exactly from what spot on the court you hit the ball, in what direction the ball went, where it landed. You want to find out what your errors were during a match, because winning tennis is a game of reducing errors. Often players who are charted for the first time are quite surprised. Maybe they can slug the ball off their forehand, but just have a defensive little chip off their backhand and they say, "If only I had a backhand, I could kill these guys." Then they're charted, and find out they miss 16 fancy forehands for every missed backhand.

Charting will help you get a good look at who you are as opposed to who you *think* you are. The correlation is often completely at odds. Once you get the message and are willing to believe it, you'll know what to do in practice. Sessions should be controlled, based on what the charts tell you about your losing points. Maybe most of your forehands from a particular spot were going wide and it was therefore evident that you needed to practice rotating the ball with more topspin. This is the kind of honest self-appraisal that is required if you're going to last in top-flight competition. Jack Kramer, for example, was always working on the weak part of his game. Even though he had just won, if a certain part of his game had failed him, he'd be out there after the match practicing a hundred of those shots. He couldn't stand going to the showers knowing he had a weakness. He kept drilling, and kept showering. Kramer was one of the cleanest people I ever knew.

Tennis is a game of consistency—being able to keep the ball in play and waiting for an opportunity—so it is important to know what your strengths are as well as your weaknesses. Some work so hard on their weak strokes that they don't maintain their strong side. This is a mistake that developing players are apt to make, and I would urge you to avoid it. In match play you work on maintaining your strong strokes as well as on developing your weak ones.

In practice sessions, always use targets that show whether you're getting depth, because depth is the name of the game. Another thing that's effective during practice is an "immediate stimulus-response mechanism"—or penalty, if you prefer. For instance, to practice deep shots I'll lay down a clothesline five feet inside the base line at both ends of the court, and then the rule is that my partner and I can't rally unless we get our shots into this five-foot zone. If it doesn't land there, we stop the rally and start over. It can get mighty frustrating if you don't work hard. Remember, the principle behind it is to keep your opponent deep, which is something Chris Evert, for example, does well. If you can pin your opponent to the base line, he can't move you more than three steps to the left or right of center; if he gets to mid-court, he can move you five to seven steps; and, if he gets to the net, he can move you eight or ten.

Another drill I like is to set tennis-ball cans on the court and actually play a match. I can't take responsibility for the insurance problems this creates, but the idea is to try to hit a can and automatically win the point. Put one in each corner, four feet in, and maybe four more in the service court to define an area. This will let you know in a hurry that it isn't strategy that wins points, it's strokes.

Which strokes are most important in a tournament competitor's arsenal? I won't have space to get into refinements, but surely four are predominant — the serve, the return of serve, the approach and the volley. So let's review how to strengthen shot production based on this sequence.

Does self-analysis show you are getting 60 to 70 percent of your first serves in, and at a decent speed? Can you throw a slice serve at an opponent with a strong forehand? And serve deep into the backhand corner to an opponent with a weak backhand? Does your second serve maintain speed?

If the answer to any of the above is "no" (or even if it's "yes"), again the key to practicing is to set up targets. On a slice serve, the slice really has to break, so set your target between five feet and ten feet inside the side line. Then try to break the ball hard with some speed and run your opponent way out of the doubles alley to return serve. For a serve into the backhand, set up a zone three feet square in both service courts. And don't forget to improve your second serve; otherwise, your opponent will run around the backhand and hit the forehand. If your opponent is able to hit a topspin forehand at your feet (which he can do on a timid serve even if he's late), it puts too much pressure on your first serve to know that you'll be in deep trouble on the second if it doesn't make it. You need to have great confidence on your second serve, as well as on your first.

Another important aspect of the serve is to be able to conceal what you're going to deal to your opponent. A savvy opponent will see where your toss goes; e.g. if it's to the server's left and he's a righty, then a twist is coming, if it's to the right, it will be a slice, and if it's to the middle and toward him, it's going to come fairly flat. Learn to serve all three from a toss just to the right of your head (for a righty).

The toss brings up the subject of the American Twist, which sacrifices speed to get rotation, and makes the ball jump big. Because the ball is tossed so far to your left, your shoulder doesn't turn, and the power comes solely from arm and wrist. For this reason, the elbow takes tremendous punishment. Better to turn your trunk, followed by the forearm and then the wrist. Not only will this save your elbow, but you can get only so far on a big-kick serve in top competition. A good player will take the service after it kicks and jump on it, often beating the server to the net. There has to be a strong relationship between speed and kick, and I think it's wiser to maintain more speed and less kick.

A good serve will come only after incalculable hours of practice, but it's worth getting right, because it's the only stroke in tennis over which you have full control. When you walk up to the line with a serving reputation in upper-echelon tennis, you command immediate respect. A big serve allows you to take more opportunities; you can gamble a bit more, because you know you're in control with your own serve. Most club players hold back because they feel that even if they break serve, they're no cinch to win their own serve. It works the other way too—once your serve is broken, psychologically you suspect you're not going to win. Yet, strangely, most people will go out and rally with their forehand ground stroke before a match, and then try a few serves just before they're ready to play. But the forehand is actually the third shot in a game; the serve is the first hit, and that's the one you should practice most on. The third shot isn't going to do much good until you have the first two down pretty darn well.

If you don't have a commanding serve, then you are obliged to possess an outstanding service return. The return of service is the second most important shot in tennis. An example is Ken Rosewall, who does not have a good serve, but is so adept at the return that he is able to reduce the advantage that big-serving opponents have against him.

On the service return, you need to take a comparatively short swing. Practice punching through the ball. The best players have a racket that finishes up high. But most important in practice is to be able to hit most of your returns back. On this stroke, be sure to practice against players with exceptional and varied serves—hard and flat ones, twists, slices, and serves from lefties. Otherwise you still won't be able to respond to the big serve. The idea is to get most, if not all, of them back, and worry about placement later.

Jack Kramer answers people who complain that they're not hitting the ball at their opponent's feet, "You're not hitting at the guy's feet, waist, chest, or head. In fact, if you watch closely, you're not even returning it." The point is that you've got to give your opponent more opportunties to lose, and you can't do that when you hit the ball into the net. If you hit the ball long, your opponent might give you a good call, but if you hit the ball into the net, only a sadist is going to say, "Super shot!"

Set those targets up where you want your return to go, and then practice, practice, and practice again. You've just got to pay your dues; if you can't do it, you have to practice returns until you can.

As for the stroke itself, there are five elements to keep in mind: (1) Take a much shorter swing. (2) Have a firm grip when you hit the ball. (3) Eye contact has to be held as long as possible. (4) Finish high on the stroke. And, (5) don't let the face of the racket get off the line of flight of the ball. In other words, a short stroke with the elbow high, and with the face of the racket aligned between you and the target.

Now, at last, we can come to the approach shot—the third most important shot in a player's arsenal. Remember, when you're working on forehand and backhand ground strokes, all you're doing is trying to keep the ball deep while waiting for the first short ball. Intermediates will get a short ball almost immediately, but top players will take a bit longer—the third, fourth or fifth shot. If you're not the first one to hit a short shot, then it's got to be your opponent. In the famous Borg vs. Vilas WCT match a few years back where the ball went across the net sometimes over 80 times during a rally, in four out of five of those shots neither needed more than three steps to get to the return. They weren't getting pushed around that quickly. But the idea is that eventually *someone* simply made a careless shot—a short ball—which allowed his opponent to run him out of the court.

And, if you are presented with a short ball, you had better be able to execute an effective approach, because theoretically the point is as good as over. So put those cans up, take some short balls off the machine, and go deep into the backhand corner. The reason to go to the backhand is that, with his forehand, your opponent can pass you diagonally cross-court—he's got about 62 feet of room—but very few players can do it off their backhand. You might say, "Sure, but isn't the guy going to *know* you're going into his backhand on every shot?" The answer is yes—but you don't care. If his backhand gives you an easy setup, what's the difference if he sets you up every time? What do you care whether he knows it or not, and he knows you know he knows, or everybody knows?

If your approach shot is good and deep, you'll win almost every point, against nearly anyone on the entire globe. Backhands and forehands are to keep the ball deep at the base line. Then wait for the first short ball from your opponent and throw it back deep to the backhand, go to the net, and it's all over. But not if your approach shot is crummy.

If you hit a short approach shot, it's like throwing up a hand grenade and running underneath it. You can't hit a short shot and then rush the net because you're not going to have any reaction time.

There's a number of other considerations that should be mentioned before space runs out. The first is that when you're trying to make the jump from club player to bigger things, you have to be able to pass well down the line. Here again, some hard practice—what else?—is called for. Have a person hit crosscourt and run into the net, then you try to hit down the line. Or have a ball machine come across at you and you keep running over to the ball and try to pass down the line. Against less-than-top-quality players you could go three feet from the side line, but against tougher competition you're going to have to hit within 24 inches.

Another thing a club player is going to have to improve upon in how to attack the net, because unless you have a super ground game like Evert or Borg or Solomon or Vilas, you have to get aggressive lest you lose on bad breaks.

Most intermediates serve and just go like crazy to the net. The trouble is one foot is ahead of the other when their opponent hits the ball, so they can't turn the corner to get the diagonal service return. The solution, of course, is to have your feet together just as the return is being hit, see which way it's going, and then take off again. Naturally, you will have liked to get as close as possible to the net by this time. To see how this is done best, watch John Newcombe if you can. He doesn't have the greatest ground strokes, but he serves very deep. Then notice what happens next; by the time he has taken his third step—the one that brings his feet together—he very often has come within a foot of the service line. Then, when his opponent has just hit the return of service, Newcombe takes off again and gets well into the service court when he makes his volley. The average person gets caught in his feet and volleys at mid-court. The drill here, then, is to measure your strides after you serve, trying to increase their length without feeling uncomfortable or uncoordinated, so that when you do bring your feet together and then start your forward motion again, you're well into the net.

All players who are starting to think bigger should be able to go to the net when they have to and be able to stay back and be patient when they have to. But here's where a club player is apt to have additional troubles; he cannot play a short game well against a good service returner. A good returner will hit the ball at the feet of the onrushing server. The aspiring player has to be able to take that ball on the volley or half-volley and lay it back deep into the base line away from his opponent's strong side. This is where most people will lose against the good service return—they can't muscle back the low ball. Now they're caught on top of the net as the opponent is hitting the ball almost a second sooner, and of course his angle is wider. The volley is the shot that separates the men from the boys. If you don't have that shot and you're a net rusher, you're just about dead against people with good service returns. So practice (someone hitting topspin and underspin shots at your feet or, it you're alone, a ball machine hitting fairly hard shots at your feet will do), taking the volley or half-volley and putting it deep into either corner. In the end, you will find that tennis is simply a game of hitting a target, and that the better players will be able to hit those targets more consistently while under the stress of competition.

A further refinement the club player should attend to is how well he reacts to a net rusher. Start keeping records of your service return at 30-all because that's the critical part of a game. A good player will return just as well at 30-all and deuce as on the first and second points. When your opponent does get to the net at this point, you've got to be able to hit a crosscourt passing shot or go down the line. To keep the ball sufficiently close to either sideline, you've only got two or three degrees leeway to pass somebody effectively. Most club players can't thread the needle that finely. And, of course, you have to be able to call on a reliable lob at times, thus taking the net completely away from the rusher.

All the foregoing will, if practiced sufficiently, add up to an improved and well-rounded game. Unfortunately, space precludes going into many of the other details of performance and finesse that top-level tennis demands, but anyway there are enough of them to fill a book (*Tennis for the Future,* by me—in case you want a reference). Basically, what it comes down to is a simple rule; hit the ball where the other guy isn't. To do this effectively, you have to possess the strokes; tennis isn't a game of strategy, it's a game of strokes.

But in tough competition you can't merely deal out strokes blindly. Just as *you* chart yourself to find out who you are, you should take the trouble to chart your opponent and find out who *he* is, what his strengths and weaknesses are. Make it your business to chart people you're determined to beat. Here are some key factors to watch for:

1) How can you tell where your opponent is apt to serve? Charting will reveal his tendencies, and get you a fast first step and maybe two on the service return so you can lean into the ball, and put it back at the feet of the server if he's rushing.

2) When you're serving find out whether to focus on your opponent's forehand or backhand.

3) When you're serving and elected to come to the net, which side is your opponent apt to try to pass you on? You want to reach a position halfway between the net and the service line, and about three feet to the right of the center stripe (if you've hit to the backhand of a righty). Then you're ready to move in for a volley at the net (so that your follow-through almost crosses the net). Anticipating where the drive may be aimed will get you those two steps forward.

4) When you go to the net against your opponent's backhand, is he going to lob or drive? If he's going to lob, you want to be able to get *back* three quick steps to the service stripe. When you get to that spot, you're not going to get lobbed over your head.

5) Determine how to break up your opponent's rhythm. Can you get him out of his troove by slowing down play or speeding it up, or mixing little floaters into a series of hard drives?

By studying and charting opponents, you'll soon find out that every player in the tennis world telegraphs his or her play, and has certain patterns. Perhaps he hits one way from the deuce court, another from the ad court, or points a toe, or holds his head at an angle. Some people, for example, will raise the elbow of their racket arm if they are going down the line. You need only one such tip-off to gain an advantage, so watch for patterns very carefully.

Finally, there is an overall piece of advice to take with you on your quest of worlds to conquer; hit the shot you have to hit, win or lose, and be proud of it. No matter what the score, don't change your game. Don't look for sophisticated strategies—they don't exist. When you're on the baseline, there's little to do except keep it deep; you can hit the corners, but that's no great mystery. When your opponent comes to the net, you have to be able to lob well, hit down-the-line passing shots, or short-angle cross-courts.

And that's really all there is to the game. Hit 'em where they ain't, as Wee Willie Keeler used to say. But the question is—*can* you hit there? The targets tell the story.

"There is an overall piece of advice to take with you on your quest for worlds to conquer: hit the shot you have to hit, win or lose, and be proud of it. No matter what the score, don't change your name . . .

INFLUENCE OF THE BIG GAME

By

Joe Walsh
University of Minnesota

It is questionable that anything really new has come into the game of tennis since Dwight Davis and Holcombe Ward, champion of 1904, worked out the American Twist service as undergraduates at Harvard before 1900, and introduced it into early cup matches with surprising results.

"Certainly there is nothing in the tennis of the 1960's that would have started the world in the year that the Titanic met the iceberg. The serving, smashing, volleying game of McLaughlin and Borotra is the game of Kramer and Gonzales." (Al Laney, *Tennis Illustrated Annual*)

It seems to be the consensus of many tennis authorities that it is difficult to say any one change is the most significant development in tennis in the past 50 years. In a book written at the turn of the century, the Doherty brothers referred to the practice of running in on service and volleying everything, and added that Oliver Campbell, the U.S. Champion of 1890, 1891 and 1892, "started this game in America, and Americans in general adopt it." They also said that Campbell would "take the ball on the rise as he dashed into the forecourt."

The Dohertys wrote their book about 20 years before Jack Kramer was born and it included the following statement: "The Americans themselves say that excessive running in on the service rather spoils the game and the server has too great an advantage." Does that sound familiar in today's tennis world? It seems that the coined phrase, big game, the so-called serve and volley type of tennis we see used by all good players today, was attributed to Jack Kramer in the early 1940's. However, as we have tried to show with small bits of history, tennis did see the big game advocates as early as the 1900's.

The big game was continued with players like Willmer Allison, John Doeg, and Vinnie Richards in the 1920's and 30's showing the same type of serve and volley game associated with this term. Perhaps the best way to consider this point is to say that Kramer might have been responsible for starting the standardization of the big game. As Chet Murphy, the former California coach and now Broadmoor tennis professional, stated: "The classic match between Kramer and Frankie Parker (a great groundstroker) on grass at Forest Hills in 1947 might have been a great turning point." Interestingly enough, John Barnaby the well-known Harvard coach and past president of the United States Professional Association, said: "Every good player today plays the same way." It does seem fairly well established that with the fast courts and the speed of today's tennis ball—all good players do play and serve and volley type of game. Unless a player is on a slow clay court, and now with the influence of the indoor courts and slow synthetic surfaces, he will not be able to compete too long in high caliber tennis without playing the so-called big game.

A brief description of what we would consider the big game would be the following: A player moves into the net directly behind the first or second serve into the so-called T area (Diagram 1) where both the center service line and the service line meet, to hit the first volley or half-volley. Then he will continue to move in and cut the second volley off with a good angle placement. In order for a player to do this effectively, the service must be considered, the movement into the court behind the service, the bounce stop or stopping position, and the volley and theory of volleying behind the service. A complete philosophy of thinking offensively and taking charge of the situation are necessary. Perhaps Kramer himself stated it best: "Attack. That one word in our estimation sums up the best execution of championship tennis."

The standardization of the big game is what we consider to be the most important change in tennis over the past 50 years. We will attempt to consider some of the technical aspects involved in the type of game.

An advanced player must keep the ball toss, weight transfer, and wrist snap in mind when he is considering the obvious points of power and control in serving. It is obvious, that in order to get power and advance to the net behind the serve, he must toss the ball in front of his body so the weight transfer will automatically be brought into the ball. When the weight transfer is shifted to the front foot and the server is rising on his toes and leaning into the ball with his entire body, then he can get the maximum reach and power. As Les Stofen stated in his philosophy on serving, a player must "trigger the wrist." Talbert stated on several occasions that the wrist snap is the heart of the serve. The server's movement should be fluid and have a smooth rhythm. It should not be an awkward action but should flow and continue to accelerate until the point of contact where the racket is given its maximum thrust upward and forward.

Spin is a vital consideration in the case of the advanced player who intends to progress to the net following his service. The flat (or cannonball) service can be a great weapon if the player has the control to get this ball into the box with good depth and placement. Sheer power is fine as long as a player knows where the ball is going . A great fast ball pitcher in baseball would always be the tough player to beat—if he could get the ball over the plate. However, when the pitcher is in real trouble and the control is not there, he will most likely go to the curve ball, because it may be more predictable and give him a greater percentage to keep the ball in the strike zone. The tennis player can learn something from the analogy. By all means he should go to the cannonball service if he can. Remember, it is necessary to have something approaching 75 to 80 per cent of the first serves that should go in. However, even Gonzales started to use spin and slice as the years went on and lost some of the effectiveness of his power on the service. Spin gives the player time to move into the T area to volley. The flat or cannonball service does not provide the time necessary to move into the forecourt to volley properly, and the player is constantly in the half-volley or volleying up position.

Spin can be developed by moving the racket upward in order to impart top and sidespin to the ball. A player can lead with the top right edge of the racket (right-handed player). Another way of saying this is the path of the racket from its cocked position is slightly from the left to right, accompanied by a late but powerful snap of the wrist and straightening of the elbow. To slice the ball, it should be placed more to the right of the head and hit on the upper right side of the ball (Illustration 3). Assuming the good slice serve is hit with both sidespin and topspin, the player should have time to get into the T area to volley. Of course, the consideration of depth and placement becomes most important in this type of situation. This is important in order to play an attacking style of game and think offensively.

A Few Tips Which Relate to Service

Grip: Use the backhand or Continental grip to get full potential of the wrist snap. We teach mainly the Continental to emphasize as little grip change as possible on all strokes.

Stance: The player should stand as close to the center line as possible for the service to the forehand box. Serving to the advantage or backhand box, a player will usually stand about three feet to the left of the center mark.

Knee Bend: Almost all of the better servers on the international scene today seem to have knee bend in the early phase of the toss (Illustration 2). This seems to play a role in building up explosive power to add to the acceleration of the swing at the point of impact. It helps in the thrust upward for vertical lift when contact is made with the ball.

Hit Up and Reach: This is used for depth and control, and also gives the player the full potential of his angle of trajectory.

Note how the server brushes up and around the ball to create spin on the serve.

Push Off the Front Foot: This action helps a player get his full thrust into the ball, and is also important in helping him get into the court in order to volley. It is the last part of the action in serving.

Service Depth and Placement in Singles: Diagram 2 shows the recommended percentages where to hit the ball on the serves. They should vary

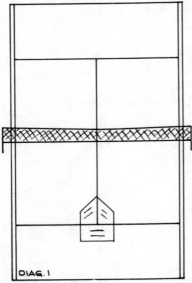

#1. "T" Area for bounce—stop on 1st volley

#2. The recommended percentage on where to hit the ball on the serve.

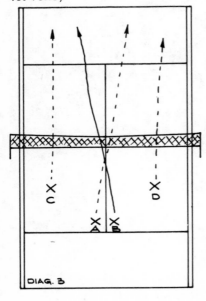

#3. Placement of volley in 4 court positions.

160

when the other player has an obvious weakness. The diagram is based on the premise that the opponent is fairly well-balanced off both sides.

The first running step into the court should be taken with the right foot (right-handed players) with the natural flow and body weight transfer into the ball (Illustration 4). Then the server is into a natural running style which can lead him to the T area where he comes into a bounce stop action to get balance and control of his body. Now he will be in good position to handle the first volley situation. Many players fail to come to this complete stop as they are executing the first volley. They try to run through the volley, and thus lack the balance and control to have some feel or finesse on the volley. The bounce stop action is imperative in order to maintain control of the body and to give the player some proper placement and control when hitting the volley. Therefore, the sequence is serve and run, bounce stop, and then volley or half-volley. We recommend that a player start to come to a bounce stop position just as he sees the opponent starting to take the final phase of his backswing.

The first volley should be hit deep and somewhat cross-court (Diagram 3). Too often in singles, players try to do too much with the first volley. Often the player will try to get too much angle, and, as a result, the shot falls far short and leaves a tremendous angle for the opponent on his return. However, if the player who is volleying hits the first return cross-court, then he is in a good position to do whatever he wishes on the second ball. The cross-court volley can be the big pay-off on the vital points.

A high school or college player should concentrate more on good depth and placement on the first volley and then move in to get better angle on the second ball. The really fine volleyer must know how to volley both deep and short, but that comes with experience and confidence. The great volleyers know that position is most important in volleying, and, therefore, they do not put away the first volley every time. They will go for the deep cross-court, except on the very weak return, and then see the great court position open for them on the second shot.

The main points we try to stress in volleying are: 1) Stay with one grip. We usually recommend the Continental grip. The one grip theory can often help eliminate some confusion. 2) Keep the racket head high. Do not allow the racket head to drop—keep it up at all times. A player might open the racket face on several balls, but the head of the racket can still remain up (Illustrations 7 and 8). 3) Squeeze at the point of contact to get full control and feel. The only time a player should relax his wrist more is when he is dealing with the touch volley. 4) A slight bend in the knees at contact seems to help because it brings the player closer to eye level to the ball, and gives him the feeling of hitting down somewhat on the ball. 5) A most important part of the volley is the execution of the cross-over step at contact to get full potential of the punching action (Illustration 8). 6) Try to get the feeling of biting

Illustration #1

Illustration #2

Illustration #3

Illustration #4

Illustration #5

Illustration #6

Illustration #7

Illustration #8

the ball at contact. A slight lead with the lower edge of the racket once contact is made will give the player a little more feel on the volley. 7) The last point is something that Bill Price, the great St. Louis teaching professional, has always stressed: "...hit the volley." If the player starts in the proper position with the racket head in front of his body and well controlled, he can take a nice little action and hit the ball.

A few of the finer points on the volley concern the low ball. When he makes contact, the player should take a little off on the low ball. Play it easy. Be soft. By spreading his feet when bending, the player will be able to cover more space and have better ability to execute. He must open the racket face slightly on the low ball in order to get adequate net clearance. On the high ball, the player should take charge of the ball and execute the cross-over step to cover the ball right away. He should not be too sharp coming down on the ball, because this often leads to poor depth, and the opponent's next shot will cause trouble. By being more concerned about depth and placement, too much power is not needed. John Bromwich, a mathematician, wrote an article entitled, "The Mathematics of Tennis." He showed by mathematical equations that when a player is in the volleying position, and he receives a volley that pulls him well off-center, he will volley down-the-line on his return. The good player knows that the short angle ball should be volleyed back down-the-line in order to get proper position for the next shot (Diagram 3).

From a technical standpoint, we have tried to cover the big game. Perhaps there was no one significant change in the past 50 years in tennis; however, most authorities do feel that all players today are playing the big game. We have concluded that the most significant change in tennis in the 50-year period is the standardization seen in the tennis world today. That is, all good players today do play the big game.

"The great volleyers know that position is the most important factor in volleying, and therefore, they don't put away the first volley every time."

ARE YOU A VICTIM OF TENNIS MYTHS?

By

Dennis Van der Meer
Tennis Professional

Whoever has taken a lesson from a teaching pro almost certainly has a roll call of cliches ringing in his ears. "Keep the racket head above the wrist." "Hit the ball well out in front of your body." "Get your racket back as soon as you see where the ball is coming from." And that most venerable of all teaching directives, "Watch the ball!"

I have been a tennis teacher for more than 20 years now, and admit to having uttered these and just about every other glib phrase at one time or another. It was a litany passed on from tennis teacher to tennis teacher, and most of us didn't think twice about it.

Curiously, through most of these years my students never complained. They were mainly youngsters, and fortunately they had the innate sense to put my good advice to use and to ignore my bad advice. If they became skilled players, it was because they got to hit a lot of balls, not because they memorized a lot of words. Some of my students became national champions, some even world champions—and, of course, yours truly became known as a very good teacher of tennis! It can go to one's head very quickly.

But eventually my teaching emphasis changed and I began to take on more adults as students. I soon discovered that I and my trite expressions were in trouble. Adults didn't swallow things whole; they asked more questions, they analyzed, they challenged. Most of all they demanded fast results. As tennis instruction grew more sophisticated in response to this demand, it became obvious to me that the old set of rules we teaching pros had relied on for years were no longer valid—and in fact were downright wrong! We would have to re-evaluate our methods.

Soon after the dawning of this realization, several fellow teachers and I go together and ran down the list of cliches. The result was the preparation of a practical teaching manual for the Professional Tennis Registry of the United States. Following are some of the "truths" that we questioned and found wanting. Now, I hope, they are on their way to the garbage dump. It's understandable that they will sound familiar to you, but the time has come to look again and see if you have been done in by old myths that are dying hard.

"Watch the ball" was the first to go. Watch the ball and see it go right past your racket and all the way to the back fence! As a helpful piece of instruction, the phrase only has meaning if it is translated to add: "Prepare early and adjust your feet so that you will be able to meet the ball dead-center on the racket face." For a student struggling to sort out all the do's and don'ts of tennis technique, that's a lot more helpful.

Here are some more antiquated assumptions that should no longer be accepted (shown in italics), with a photo and brief description of the way things *really* should be:

Incorrect   **Correct**

1) *Keep the racket head above the wrist.* Wrong. Just maintain the angle between your forearm and the racket throughout each individual stroke. Under these conditions your racket head will correctly be above the wrist on high shots, and below the wrist on low ones.

2) *Come over the ball for topspin.* Don't. The best way to hit topspin is to come up from behind the ball and finish with the racket travelling from low to high, keeping the racket face perpendicular to the ground.

3) *Get your racket back the moment you see the ball coming.* Nope. The first thing to do is to turn your shoulders the moment you see the direction of the return. *Then* get the racket back.

Incorrect   **Correct**

Incorrect   **Correct**

4) *Turn your side to the net.* Do not turn your whole body sideways. Just turn your shoulders and pivot.

5) *Meet the ball waist high.* This is OK for some people, particularly those with low waists. Most players, however, should ideally meet the ball at thigh level.

 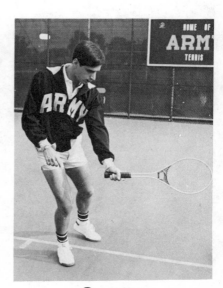

Incorrect   **Correct**

Incorrect   **Correct**

6) *Transfer your weight from your back foot to your front foot as you hit the ball.* The weight should be transferred *before* you hit the ball. The power of the stroke comes from hip and shoulder rotation.

7) *For a powerful serve, snap your wrist over the ball.* Do not try to break your wrist to get on top of the ball. The correct serving motion will come from rotating wrist and forearm forward.

Incorrect   **Correct**

8) *The topspin lob is a low-percentage shot.* The next television commentator who perpetuates this myth should be strung up with cat gut. Club-level players should be encouraged to come under and up on the ball when they lob. Then even if the lob falls short, it will take a very experienced opponent to hit a winning smash off the spinning, fast-dropping ball.

9) *Come around the ball for a slice serve.* That's not so much wrong as it is misleading. It suggests that the racket goes from left to right and is sort of wrapped around the ball. Perhaps a better phrase would be "bypass" the ball.

Incorrect   **Correct**

Incorrect   **Correct**

10) *The racket is an extension of the hand.* As wrong as it is to try to cock the wrist, it is equally wrong to lower the wrist in an effort to make the racket line up with the hand. On the forehand side, the racket comfortably makes an angle of about 120° with the forearm, while for the backhand it is as closed as 90°.

11) *Don't hold your thumb up the handle for the backhand.* The thumb will add considerable security and stability to the grip. Be sure, though, that the knuckles are not placed on the top of the handle, which can cause a jabbing type of stroke.

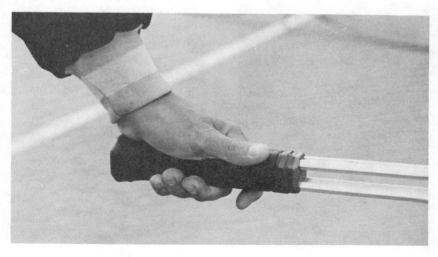

12) *Don't play in no-man's land.* The service line area supposedly marks a danger area where you will be caught out of position, but in doubles you cannot protect against the opposing net player unless you are stationed there. So the student might as well learn to play and react in this zone as well.

13) *Hit the ball far out in front your body.* Hitting the ball too far out in front is as bad as hitting it too late. There is an optimum point of contact relative to the grip, and any contact point away from it—in front or in back—will not bring the best results.

Incorrect

Correct

Other ill-conceived theories that are making their way to the tennis graveyard are:

14) *Good players don't change grips.* Well, I have my own response to that: doodly squat! A tournament-level player changes grips often, but because the shift may be quite subtle he will swear he didn't. In reality, the grip changes by slight repositioning of the hand, varying the pressure of the fingers, and pivoting the wrist and elbow.

15) *A straight backswing is quicker than a continuous semi-circular backswing.* Once you have made your initial shoulder turn, simply lowering the racket in a small arc is faster than taking it straight back.

16) *Inexperienced players can't learn the correct service grip.* Beginners may *briefly* use the straight forehand grip for the serve, but by learning to hit up at the ball, even a novice can and should master the correct service grip.

17) *Players with weak arms should learn the two-handed backhand.* This is dangerous nonsense. Only someone nursing a tennis elbow or who is very talented should employ this stroke. How will the playing arm ever get stronger if it's always in a brace?

18) *You need a highly developed "touch" to learn the drop shot.* Not so. Even very inexperienced players should use this shot. It is quite easy to learn when it is presented as the same motion as the volley.

TACTICS AND COACHING

11

TENNIS AND MENTAL PRACTICE

By

Steven A. Weiss
Fenton High School, Bensenville, Illinois

Mental practice refers to the symbolic rehearsal of a physical activity in the absence of any gross muscular movements. Within the last ten years, there has been a marked increase of interest in this area, with many research studies conducted to determine the value of mental practice in the acquisition of a perceptual motor skill.

Three basic groups, the physical practice group (PP), the mental practice group (MP), and the no practice group (NP) are most commonly employed to compare the differences between the initial physical performances of each group and the final physical performances. The PP group is the only one that practices physically the skill to be acuired. The MP group rehearses the skill in imagination for periods of time ranging from one minute in some studies to 30 minutes in others. The NP group is given strict instructions not to practice the skill in any way during the study interval.

The results of most of these studies have indicated that mental practice procedures are associated with improved performance in the task, mental practice facilitates the acquisition of a skill, and when mental practice and physical practice trials are alternated during the acquisition of a skill, the improvement in performance will be as good or better than only the physical performance trials.

During the past year, we devised and put into use a system which included mental practice in our tennis coaching program. It was found that in early learning stages mental practice could be utilized to develop the specifics of the tennis skills to be learned, and, in effect, produce good habits instead of bad ones. This is based on the physiological fact that the process of imagining a movement is associated with the presence of action currents in the muscle groups which are used in making the actual movements. Neural patterns become strengthened through mental practice and motor responses in turn become reinforced while neuromuscular coordination is facilitated.

The latter was particularly true of the freshmen athletes who did not have very much previous tennis experience. However, the varsity players had developed stroke habits, and found it more difficult to break the bad ones and substitute better skill specifics in their place. By the same token, mental practice helped those boys who had acquired bad habits by making them concentrate more on each specific part of the tennis stroke or skill with which they had difficulty.

We also found that mental practice could be employed more effectively when the component parts of a skill were taught with associated reference points. As an example, in teaching the ground strokes, we demonstrated the specific techniques and applied them to a batter swinging at a baseball. Then the tennis players would go through each specific and visualize themselves in their mind's eye actually going through the entire stroke one step at a time and picture how they would hit a basebll in a related manner. Similarly the serve can be taught as simulating a baseball pitcher in the sequence of the ready position, cocked arm, the throw or hit, and the follow through. The tennis volley may also be likened to a bunt in baseball or a jab punch in boxing.

Each day the tennis player should practice in his mind the specifics of each of the strokes, incorporating the similarities mentioned as reference points. Then he should perform each stroke a set number of times in his mind's eye and report his mental progress to the coach. A form can be used to keep permanent progress records if it is desired. The coach should note each boy's progress and encourage him to increase the amount of mental practice when he feels he is ready.

Mental practice can also be used during the actual physical practice. A short period of time might be allowed for the players to execute the skills mentally, especially after the teaching of a new tennis technique. Pre-season training is an excellent time to utilize mind rehearsal as a review and to get the players thinking about tennis techniques.

It is difficult to say at this stage whether or not the players would have progressed as well if they had not practiced mentally. However, from our observations of this coaching technique and the favorable comments from the participants, as compared to having coached tennis without mental practice, we feel this form of practice was a definite asset to our tennis program. Based on the fact that mental practice is physiologically sound and substantiated by research, it is logical to assume that more and more coaches should experiment with this technique.

The implications of mental practice and athletic performance are many. For instance, if more and more evidence supports the hypothesis that mental practice can take the place of some of the time spent in physical practice, then more practice time could be utilized for the discussion and planning of strategy, reviewing past performances, etc. There is a definite value in mental practice for sports which require outdoor practice such as tennis, golf and baseball. Indoor mental activity could simply substitute for lost outdoor practice.

Mental practice may well become a revolutionary new coaching technique where mind rehearsal methodology will be adapted for every sport in much the same way that manuals and books have been written describing the physical performances and skill techniques involved in each sport.

THINK MINI-COURT!

By

Vince Eldred
Tennis Professional

Too often tennis coaches and pros exhort a pupil to keep his eye on the ball, believing this to be the cure-all for tennis errors. It might be better to urge the players to keep the ball in play and not take unnecessary and/or risky shots. It is true that not watching the ball is one cause of errors. After a few practice sessions, however, even the beginner watches the ball closely, and is still prone to needless errors. This is due to a failure to keep a point or rally going.

An important facet to winning tennis is consistency. William T. Tilden, one of the greatest players of all time, claimed that 70 per cent of all points are won by errors, and 30 per cent from outright winning shots. The errors are balls hit into the net, or out. Here, we are concerned with errors resulting in shots that are hit out. Additionally, Tilden urges, keep the ball in play and give the opponent another shot at it.

Many players are impatient and impetuous, attempting to win a point with a spectacular shot; aiming at the line, instead of biding their time and keeping the rally going until a reasonable opening is presented. According to Bill Talbert, formerly ranked second in the United States, to make errors, however spectacular, leads to naught; but to keep the ball under control and in play leads to victory over many an opponent.

When players, particularly world class players, do hit the baseline or sideline, spectators believe that they aim for these lines. There is a saying among players, however, that goes something like this: If I hit the line, I'm lucky. But, if my shot is in six inches or a foot, I'll take credit for a good shot. The master tennis player plays into a minicourt (Diagram 1): a court within the true court. This is to allow for an error in judgement, and to provide a safety margin for all of the shots.

Everyone makes errors, including the professional or expert player. The top player, however, is able to control the shots to the extent that the ball consistently lands within a few feet of the target area. To make allowances for the few feet, the player pictures a mini-court which provides a safety margin.

The distances of the mini-court lines from the true court lines should be determined by the skill and experience of each player. The beginner or in-

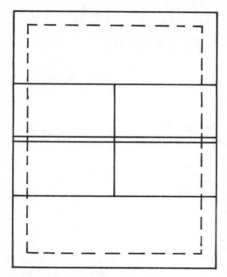

The line made up of dashes indicates the mini-court, the court within the true court. Visualize the mini-court when playing. It affords a safety margin, vital to good tennis.

termediate player obviously has less control of the shots than the expert. Due to inexperience, the beginner may, for example, visualize the mini-court five or more feet within the true court. The intermediate, with more ability and experience, establishes the court within a court commensurate with his talent for ball control. Most players have a tendency to hit long shots over or beyond the baseline. Hence, a slightly greater safety margin along that baseline may be necessary than along the sideline area.

Assuming that the beginning player pictures the mini-court baseline seven feet within the true baseline, let us examine how the mini-court applies. After one or two exchanges, the player hits a ball that strikes the court within two feet of the true baseline. True, the player did exceed the mini-court limits, but the important feature is that a good, deep shot, often a winner was hit, and the ball was kept in play. Had the player not been thinking mini-court, the ball probably would have hit the backstop, or at best, landed way out of court.

Mike Davies, the British Davis Cup player, poses two questions and provides the answers: How is a tennis match won? Is it by hitting the most winners? It may be surprising to find that in any first-class match, less than half the points come from winners. The vast majority are the result of errors— balls hit into the net or outside the lines. Remember, that is in top-class competition; in ordinary competition, the proportion is higher still.

As the beginner and intermediate players acquire better ball control, and develop the ability to keep the ball in play, the mini-court should be proportionately enlarged. Regardless of how proficient a player becomes, he should never lose sight of the mini-court. It reduces errors and lends for a higher degree of consistency.

DON'T LET THE WIND GET YOU DOWN

By

Vince Eldred
Tennis Professional

Every tennis player prefers to play under ideal weather and court conditions. A smooth court, no wind, minimal sun glare, and a good background: These conditions are a player's dream. Unfortunately, one cannot have utopia all the time.

When playing under less than favorable conditions, keep in mind that the opponent is probably experiencing similar feelings. There is no choice but to make the best of a poor situation. The playing conditions are the same for both players; the winner will be the one with the better mental approach and game plan. When there is no control over the situation, it is important to have a positive mental approach.

The player must make up his mind to utilize an unpleasant feature—the wind—to his advantage. Rather than letting it get him down psychologically, a player should consider the wind a challenge. Though difficult to contend with, the wind is hardly an insurmountable obstacle. The thinking player both uses and benefits from the wind, so that the opponent is battling not one but two adversaries—the player and the elements.

Aside from the slight variations, there are basically three types of wind conditions to contend with. First, the wind that blows with the shots, carrying the best shots and lobs out of court. Secondly, the wind that blows against the player, causing otherwise excellent shots and lobs to fall short. Lastly, there is the cross-wind, resulting in anticipated backhands suddenly becoming forehands and vice versa. The most difficult is the gusty wind which, without warning, suddenly moves the ball off-course just as the player is set and ready to hit it. Unlike the other types of wind, there is no pattern for adjustment that can be used with a gusty wind.

When hitting with the wind, topspin is a player's best ally. Overspin is the only method of pulling the ball into court. In this circumstance, instead of depth, strive for pace coupled with topspin. This is an excellent passing shot and a fine baseline weapon. Spin or slice the serves for control, or they are apt to float. Lob with backspin for control. The spin tends to bite into the following wind and helps to keep the ball inside the playing court.

When hitting into the wind, do not be afraid to hit out more than usual.

The thinking player both uses and benefits from the wind, so that the opponent is battling not one but two adversaries—the player and the elements.

Obviously, there is a judgment factor involved. The degree of added pace is commensurate with the wind velocity to be counteracted. The same formula applies with lobbing for serving. The ball should be hit harder in this instance; however, do not slug the ball recklessly. Overhit just enough to compensate for the force of the wind, allowing it to bring the ball in court.

In a cross-wind, if wind carries the ball into the backhand, the shots must be adjusted accordingly. Try to place the lobs over the opponent's forehand. When hitting to his forehand, hit wider than usual, letting the wind drift the ball into the desired target area. When hitting either a backhand cross-court or forehand down the line, allow for a greater safety margin than usual; the cross-wind, left to right, will carry the normally angled shots out.

The turbulent or gusty wind is the most difficult to adjust to. To compensate, shorten the backswing on the ground strokes because it is easier to make a last second stroke adjustment should the ball be abruptly blown into or away from the body. Toss the ball lower when serving. This lessens the chances for the wind to affect the ball.

Sustained concentration is always important in tennis, but under adverse wind conditions it becomes a must. Watch the ball very closely and be prepared to move—forward, backward, or laterally—depending upon how the wind affects the flight of the ball both before and after it bounces.

Whenever the wind is a factor, modify the overall game to the situation. Use topspin when hitting with the wind; stroke with added pace when hitting against it; allow for wind drift in the cross-wind; and shorten the ground stroke backswing when the wind is gusting.

BUILDING SKILLS FOR BASIC TENNIS

By

Charles Wolbers
East Stroudsburg, Pennsylvania, State College

Would it not be wonderful if the gymnasium instructor could actually start to teach the game of tennis when he undertakes a school tennis instructional program? Many times it is simply not practical to introduce a game like tennis in the public schools where a high percentage of pupils lack the basic skills necessary to its performance. The current concern for physical fitness should help in this matter, for without a certain amount of strength, vigor, and agility the beginner will find tennis discouraging, to say the very least. There are ways of building fitness, of introducing low-net games into the physical education and play programs of youngsters, and of readying them to play tennis. There is a definite move to get the nation's youth playing tennis. To assure the success of a school or recreational program, the necessary ground work must be laid.

In public school teaching, we are always concerned with two important realities: one, the large number of pupils per class, usually with widely divergent levels of skill; two, the ever-present pressure of limited time. If we are to teach tennis successfully in schools, it seems to us that the necessity of building basic skills must be stressed. Somehow we must be sure that pupils have in their training—prior to tennis—those lead-up activities such as drills, games, self-testing activities, relays, and experiences in movement exploration which will help build the skills basic to the learning and enjoyment of the game.

These activities, by and large, do not require much equipment or tennis paraphernalia. For this, school authorities will be happy. Another reality we must face in the schools is the shortage of equipment of all kinds. School men and physical education teachers will also note that this recommendation fits in very nicely with an emphasis on physical fitness. Most of the lead-ups we could name contribute directly to the components of fitness. If we insist that this groundwork of skill be laid before we attempt to teach tennis, our job will be made easier and the tennis promotion will gain acceptance in the schools.

The situation parallels that of an English composition teacher who finds that before she can tackle the composition work, she must drill her pupils in spelling, sentence structure, and punctuation. If her students should come to her already possessing these basic English skills, she could go directly to the subject matter; that is, she could expect them to accomplish something in the way of creative writing.

What we are saying is that if youngsters come to class with a reasonable amount of skill—possessing sufficient strength, agility, coordination, and the like—the teaching of tennis can begin immediately and progress rapidly. Mass instructional techniques are being perfected for large groups of tennis pupils, but they can hardly be put into action with the present level of skill we find in youngsters. If the youngsters have been properly prepared, the teaching situation brightens considerably. In this case we can even hope to have some time for special attention to those who are above or below par. It can be hoped that everyone in the class will realize sufficient success that he may be motivated to continue playing the game. If so, he may be counted on to seek out-of-school situations in which he continues to improve his stroking, to get into some real competition. As with all things, his enjoyment of tennis may be directly measured by the degree of success he achieves. This initial exposure to the game of tennis in school presents a very great challenge to the teacher. It is up to the teacher to see that the pupil's first try is not his last.

What are some of the lead-up activities which can be advocated for school physical education programs? Here are a few areas in which work needs to be done.

First, for strength we need weight training, as distinguished from weight lifting, isometric-type contraction exercises, and heavy resistance exercises. Second, for endurance—running. Nothing develops endurance like running. Third, for hand-eye coordination—ball bouncing drills and play with paddle ball sets. Fourth, for loco-motor skills, agility, timing, footwork—may we commend the devotees of movement education and creative rhythms and dance whose work helps youngsters explore and experiment with bodily movement, develop the kinesthetic sense, probing the problems of space patterns, weight transfer, step combinations, and the like. Fifth, for familiarity with the game—games and drills which contain specific elements of tennis, popular paddle tennis, and other low-net games. Very few low-net games are being played in our schools today. Their inclusion would be an important step toward familiarizing students with tennis. A net can be suggested by a rope strung across a room or playing area. Portable net stands and nets are easily improvised.

Other sports have their complement of lead-ups; relays and kicking games for soccer, ball-handling drills and relays for basketball and baseball, and games like hit-pin which teach all the elements of baseball (played with a kicked ball, making it safer for younger aspirants to America's pastime).

Why not tennis? Any physical educator should be able to devise a program of training preparatory to tennis. The activities he plays need no special tennis equipment, and he must be mindful that they have a definite carry-over to tennis—they really build for tennis skill. If it so happens that in building for tennis his pupils should become more physically fit, more capable in other games, would not that be a happy circumstance?

Methods and techniques of teaching tennis to youngsters in school classes were the subject of a special seminar conducted at Ohio State University last October. Set up by a joint committee of the USLTA and AAHPER, the seminar involved leading American tennis mentors. The ELYA, under recently elected President Sutter, is developing plans for a series of seminars aimed at the public school teachers of tennis. This is a healthy trend; tennis has long been neglected in the physical education training institutions. The teachers in the field are eager to gain the knowledge and skills for teaching tennis to children. Tennis has been too long unavailable to the average youngster. Those who play tennis well up into the senior years would gladly submit their game as one of the finest recreational pursuits for adults. And many of them are quick to say they wish they had started to play much earlier in life.

Many adults wish they'd started to play tennis much earlier in life.

COACHING POINTS FOR TENNIS

By

Joe Walsh
University of Minnesota

Don Budge said that one of the reasons he won the Grand Slam of Tennis in 1937 was because he finally learned to take the ball on the rise. Taking the ball on the rise can be controversial when coaches discuss at what stage a player should attempt to master this coaching point. Most tennis authorities agree that taking the ball on the rise is a vital part of top class tournament tennis. A player seldom reaches the top in competition until he acquires this skill. However, a high school player may not be far enough along in the development of his game to master the skill, but he can be made aware of its value in his future development.

It is the purpose of the article to discuss a few of the key factors involved in good tennis. Some of the topics to be covered will not be new to many coaches, but perhaps emphasis is needed so they can re-evaluate their coaching duties. A coach does not always have to be an experienced player in order to get many of the coaching values across. In many high school situations across the country today, we find a tennis coach who might not have a tennis background which gives him the competency he would like to have. However, many of the things necessary in successful tennis coaching require only good common sense. We have found that even at the good collegiate level of competition, many mistakes made by college players can be found in some of the following. We are not saying the points that will be covered are always successful, but they are valid and most good players must eventually learn to understand them.

Concentration: This is a most difficult trait to establish in many young players who are just starting to make progress in tennis at the competitive level. Great concentration traits as seen in the top class players are rare. Many of our top players will often come off the court after a loss and say: "...my stem of concentration just left me at the vital time." How can a player be intense and also cool? How can he play every point—as if it is his last? How can coaches help their players get away from the so-called loose points? These are questions that must be considered when this crucial phase of tennis is being discussed. We try to use a few of the following techniques to instill better concentration in our player:

(a) VASSS Sets: The 21-point games system of scoring seems to have merit in getting away from playing the loose points. Every point is a big one in this type of scoring. The player knows he must be tough on every point or the match will be over quickly. It may often be a good policy to play some challenge matches with this system to work on the concentration factor. There is also a MAX system that is quite good for the same purpose. For information contact Lloyd Stockstad, Tennis Pro, Des Moines Racket Club, Des Moines, Iowa.

(b) One Ball Serving Games: Using just one ball for the serve for each box will help a player understand the value of getting the first ball in each time. It places added pressure on his concentration when he knows that he does not have that second ball to serve. There is great psychological edge to getting the first ball in when serving, and this type of practice is often good for the player. Also, the fact that he is only allowed one ball to serve, he cannot just serve a big soft one in, or he will be pressed by his opponent.

(c) Situation Tennis: Develop critical situations which a player will often find himself involved in during a match. Give some type of reward to the players who react better under pressure situations. Place players in "add out, 15-30, 30-15, deuce, 40-30, 30-40 situations," and see how they accept the challenge. Play some games with no service involved and no net play so the coach can work on just the baseline game for depth and placement. Try using 8 to 10 game pro sets in challenge matches to help the players learn to get into a match right away. There are many other situations coaches may wish to develop for their own situations. At any rate, if the result is more interest on the part of the player in concentration, the coach has accomplished his purpose.

Change the Game: This is a rather simple point which has been stressed throughout the years in tennis. Yet, coaches find it is often overlooked by many good tennis players. If a player learns to concentrate on the court, he should also learn to do something different on the court when he is losing. Perhaps he should use imagination. There are situations when a player may be hitting the ball quite well and have nice pace on it, but if he is being defeated and wants to win, he must change his game. Often the change is quite simple, and the result can be tremendous. Too often a coach looks for a drastic change which may not be needed. As an example, a player is playing good tennis but on his approach shots he is hitting too hard. As a result, he does not have enough time to get into the net position to volley properly. A slight change may be to slow down the approach shots, so more time will elapse before the opponent hits the ball, and as a result, the player gets a better volleying position. Perhaps the player is hitting the serve effectively in terms of speed, but is not moving the ball enough. Just simple movement of the ball and getting a little more angle now and then may be the only change needed to get him back into the match. Let us consider the following:

Concentration is a key factor in well-played tennis.

(a) Whenever a player is losing badly he should start to do something different, and soon, not when the match is over.

(b) Do something different—how? 1) Use more spin or less. 2) Use more lobs, especially in high school tennis. 3) Bring the opponent up more, or keep him back with lobs. 4) Hit both long and short and not just side to side. 5) Use more drop shots on slow courts, and then lob. 6) The player should pace himself on the court, not be in a hurry. 7) Slow down the opponent's momentum.

Stay on the Ball: There are certain class players who have amazing ball control and feel. What is this called? It is simply the ability to stay on the ball with the racket head as long as a player can. Kramer was said to be a master of staying on the ball throughout the stroke. It used to seem as though he would just decide at the last moment where to hit the ball. To the observer, he seemed to possess that amount of control. This is important for the good player to understand. By staying on the ball with the racket strings as long as he can, he will get better depth and placement on his stroke. Series A shows a player with wonderful ball control off the backhand groundstroke. Notice his fine ability to stay on the ball throughout the full stroke. When a player is able to do this, then he can get the good depth, placement, and feel on the stroke. Let the racket head do the work, and this is especially true against a hard hitter. More clay court players have developed this ability due to the need for more control in the slower clay court game. Some considerations may be as follows:

(a) A player should not pull-up short unless he wants the quick topspin angle shot. Let the strings ride through the ball until the stroke is completed.

(b) He should direct the shot and the ball and not permit the ball to direct him as the hitter.

(c) The control factor may often be influenced by the type of stringing. At the high school level we are more of the belief that nylon strung rackets should be the preference. Not only is some money saved, but we feel nylon often can lead to more feel and control. A gut strung racket will often provide the zip many players want, but most high school players should concentrate more on control. Along the same line of thinking, perhaps a racket that is strung too tight may not help the control factor. In our opinion, exceptionally tight strung rackets are often not justified.

The Serve: Hit Up on the Ball and Reach: Players must try to hit up on the serve and get the full reach. They must get good vertical lift before becoming overly concerned about bringing all the forces forward. Newton's Laws of Motion state: "...a body in motion will continue in that line of motion unless acted upon by another force." What does this mean to tennis coaches? Simply, that once the player starts action forward, he will get all forces going forward, unless he does something to alter this by another action. Coaches need not be overly concerned with the action going forward to the extent of not concentrating on the vertical lift of the service action.

Series A.

A-1 A-2 A-3

A-4 A-5

Series B.

B-1

B-2

B-3

B-4

B-5

B-6

This vertical reach provides better angle, better explosive power, and a better chance to get depth on the serve. It has been found that by getting good vertical lift, the player can get the wide angle serve easier. *Reach* is a word we use continually when our players are working on a serving drill. Even good college players tend to become lazy in not getting the full vertical reach they should attain when serving. The player will find himself not getting the big first ball in, using an excessive amount of spin on the second ball, and, as a result, he will hit too short. The reaching factor and hitting up on the ball are vital to good serving techniques. Notice the good extension of the player shown in Series B at the point of contact.

It has been the purpose of this article to introduce a few key points in coaching tennis. There are many others such as shorten the backswing, use cross-courts when in trouble, use the spin, vary the hitting levels, use the lob, use the cross-over step on the volley, have patience, and play the percentages, etc. However, it would be too lengthy to attempt to discuss each point in but one article. To say that any one is more important would not be a true statement. A coach must evaluate each player and consider the coaching points from which he may benefit.

It may be worthwhile to mention one last consideration, which is simplicity. Coaches should treat each player with the utmost respect, because of his playing ability. However, even with varsity players, keep things simple and try to get to the basic point. Simplicity, enthusiasm, and setting a challenge are three important considerations for successful coaching in any sport.

"Staying on the ball" is simply the ability to stay on the ball with the racket head as long as the player can.

191

ADVANCED COACHING POINTS FOR TENNIS

By

Joe Walsh
State University College at Brockport, New York

There are many considerations of which the tennis coach should be cognizant. In past articles we have written for *Athletic Journal* we have tried to convey several concepts that would seem to help the high school and college tennis coach. Now we would like to discuss three more advanced coaching considerations: hitting into levels, the use of spin, percentages, and patience.

Hitting Into Levels

Even today many coaches still tell young players that the ball just clearing the net by a foot or two is always the best shot. A blanket statement such as this one just does not make good tennis sense. The object of the game of tennis is to force weakness in the opponent's returning stroke. In this manner, the opponent will then hit short, and it is possible to take advantage of the short ball and attack. When a player just clears the net, he is hitting a short ball most of the time and, therefore, he does not have the necessary depth on his shot. When this occurs, the opponent has the advantage of moving in on a good approach shot.

The intention to place pressure on a man who is rallying in the backcourt can only be accomplished by something other than power, and that factor is depth. It is possible to achieve good depth by picking up the height of the net clearance on the strokes. This means simply hitting into a higher level. When a player attempts to clear the net by only a foot or two, this is often called the passing level shot. The shot is most effective when the opponent is applying pressure and the attempt to hit the passing stroke is made.

The second stroke we referred to is the groundstroke shot for getting depth on the ball, and this can be called the depth level stroke. However, there is another level in the shots from the backcourt and this is the extreme level or known as the lobbing level. If a player feels he cannot hit the passing shot or low level shot when an opponent is at the net pressuring—then the player should go to this lobbing level. This shot usually clears the net by 10 to 15 feet, depending on whether it is an offensive or defensive lob.

Chet Murphy, the former University of California coach, is the man who refers to what we have been talking about as hitting into levels. Other coaches have used different terms to describe this coaching consideration; however, hitting into levels seems to be a good way to describe exactly what is happening. Remember the three levels discussed:

A—Passing Level: Used when an opponent is coming into the net and it is desirable to keep the ball in such a position that the opponent is forced to volley up on his shots. The level is usually no higher than a 2 to 3 foot net clearance.

B—Groundstrokes for Depth Level: This is the stroke that is hit when both players are in the backcourt rallying. The ball should clear the net anywhere from 5 to 10 feet—this gives good depth on the shots and might force the opponent to hit short on his return.

C—Lobbing Level: Used when the player is in great trouble or when an opponent rushes the net and does not maintain the good balance he needs. This shot clears the net by more than 10 feet in an offensive situation. However, when under pressure or definitely in a defensive situation, the ball might clear the net by 15 to 20 feet at a time. This permits time to achieve good court position and get back into action.

One last factor to consider—there seems to be some psychological point involved when hitting into levels. By changing the level of net clearance, the player will keep the opponent guessing and does not permit him to groove his stroke.

Percentages and Patience

It is our belief that tennis for the very fine player is a game of playing the percentages and patience. Ken Rosewall again comes to mind when we consider the importance of percentages in the game of tennis. He is truly a master at having the percentage shot for all situation in the game. Rosewall certainly has the wonderful execution one would expect of the professional, but he also seems to have that little something extra when we consider the point of percentages. In order for the good varsity player to gain this attribute of playing percentage tennis, he must definitely have the patience factor to go along with this trait.

Too often we see the good college or high school player letting his patience wander at key times and instead of playing a percentage shot, he will go for the spectacular or winner. The really strong high school or college player will discipline his thinking so he will know that he must play this game with percentage tennis as his guide. He must learn to discipline his thinking in going cross-court more on passing shots, or when he wants to get better court position for the next shot. He must learn to discipline his thinking about keeping the ball deep on that second serve and cut down the angle of his opponent's return of service. He must remember to lob when in doubt, and to be a little more patient in trying to win the point. Often a player would be much better off to try to win a volley situation on two volleys instead of on the big first volley. Frequently just one more good deep shot would enable him to get that nice short ball off the opponent's return, yet how many times do we see young players who do not have the patience for the one more good deep shot to force the opponent to hit that weak ball? It must always be remembered there is a proper shot for every situation on the court when we consider percentage tennis. This does not mean that every single volley should be cross-court or that every second serve in doubles should be deep to the center, but it does mean that on crucial points the percentage game invariably is the best answer to good competitive tennis. Percentage tennis and patience cannot be separated because it is almost impossible for a good player to play the true percentage game unless he does have the patience.

A good high school coach should have chalk talks with his team on situations involved on the tennis court. He should point out the strokes that professional and good college players use in certain circumstances. What is the sound shot for the certain way to combat a situation? Is it the lob, down-the-line, cross-court, the hip, top-spin, etc.? All good players should be made aware of the thinking behind each shot and why it is executed in such situations. We find that if we will stop our player in the middle of practice sessions every now and then, and put them into situation tennis circumstances that force them to deal with percentage tennis—this can be a useful coaching technique. Play some quick 11 point games from the backcourt with no service involved for the pressure of groundstrokes and the patience factor. Steadiness can often help a player better understand the value of patience. Too many of our top college players lose this attribute they may have had in their early years or at the high school level. A good tennis player never loses the characteristics of patience, he just allows his tennis repertoire to grow in being able to do a little more with the ball. Patience never leaves the good player—and should always be a strong attribute of the successful coach.

The Use of Spin

John Barnaby, the well-known Harvard coach, states that the use of spin and slice in today's game of tennis is an important factor to great tennis. The theory of many fine tennis people has been to use as little spin as possible as long as they have what may be called controlled power. We cannot be naive and deny the use of power in tennis. It is something most great players have somewhere in their game, it may be controlled, but power is not to be taken lightly. Gonzales, Hoad, and Tilden had power; Newcomb, Smith, and Laver have power. Therefore, no tennis authority should say power (especially when controlled) is not vital to great tennis players.

However, tennis players must also use spin effectively. What does spin do? Why do we use it? Basically, spin cuts down the margin of error. Spin keeps the ball in the court and usually is better for control. Rosewall with his wonderful sidespin backhand shot is a master of using spin for control. Spin on a service give a player more time to get into the court for position and first volley situations. The cannonball serve does not allow the time element that spin does. A player might be playing against a cannonball server or a power hitter, and he may have great difficulty returning serve. He may have already been told to shorten his swing, but he is still having trouble returning. What should he do? How about using some slice or chip on the return to keep the ball in play? He is now at least on his way to getting some balls back into the court and getting some semblance of control. Following are a few good instances when we should seriously consider using spin:

A — Top-Spin: 1) On most forehands, especially cross-court when the opponent is attacking the net. 2) Top-spin on the second serve to bring the ball into the box. 3) Top-spin also gives a good high bounce that is often needed on the serve and certain groundstrokes.

B — Underspin or Slice: 1) Backhand return of serve on the high ball. 2) Hitting down-the-line on the approach shots. 3) Chip return against the cannonball serve. 4) Approach shots, because it keeps the ball low thus forcing the opponent to hit up.

Some people often refer to a player who uses excessive amounts of spin as a *junk player*. This may be true to some extent; however, to deny the good use of spin and slice in the game of tennis is to be unrealistic about what is going on in the game today at the tournament and collegiate levels. We do not feel that anyone can deny the greatness of controlled power, but spin is definitely involved in today's game. If spin is eliminated, then the great top-spin backhand of Laver, top-spin forehand of Okker, and the wonderful side-slice of Rosewell are eliminated. It is indeed rare to see any great player who can truly hit just flat off the ground today. However, notice that they almost all use spin effectively on certain shots. We cannot live in a dream world and refuse even to talk about spin; however, a few well-respected tennis men still decline even to consider this aspect of the game. It is simply fact, it is part of the game, it has been, and always will be. The sooner we recognize this fact, the better we can serve our players at the advanced level. We are saying: Spin, if used efficiently and at the right time, is vital to good tournament, high school, and collegiate tennis.

DEVELOPING FORWARD AND BACKWARD MOVEMENT

By

Hans Leis, Jr.
University of Texas at Austin

Most tennis players have excellent lateral movement, but few seem to have exceptional forward and backward movement. Developing this type of movement would benefit the player in covering lobs and drop shots. Too many overheads are missed because a player is one or two steps too slow in moving backward to get under the lob, as a rule, one hit with the wind or one hit with heavy topspin. How many times have we witnessed a player who is one or two steps too slow in moving forward to return a drop shot? As a result, he must contact the ball below the level of the net, forcing him to hit up, and thereby giving his opponent an easy return shot.

Several drills have been designed to develop forward and backward movement. One of these is the star drill (Diagram 1). In this drill the hitter faces the net at the intersection of the service line and the center line. Upon command, the hitter will run and touch his racket on the net next to the right net post. Then he will turn and run, cross his starting point, and then touch his racket on the intersection of the doubles left sideline and the baseline.

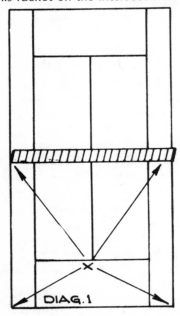

DIAG. 1

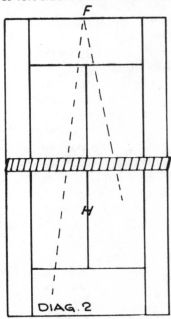

DIAG. 2

The hitter returns to his starting point, then turns quickly and runs to touch his racket at the intersection of the doubles right sideline and the baseline. Then he turns immediately, crosses his original starting point, and touches his racket on the net, next to the left net post. Finally, he returns to his original starting point. The drill can be varied by having the player run down the line from the intersections of the doubles sideline and the baseline to the net posts, rather than crossing at the intersection of the service line and the center line. Timing the player with a stopwatch can be used for motivation.

The lob and drop drill (Diagram 2) can also be used to develop good forward and backward movement. It begins with the hitter facing the center of the net at a racket's length distance. The feeder is standing at the baseline and is attempting to hit an offensive lob. Unless the hitter has very quick backward movement, he will not be able to get underneath the ball and will have to return the lob after it goes over his head and bounces. As soon as the hitter returns the lob, the feeder takes another ball and attempts to hit a drop shot, forcing the hitter to run forward to return the ball. After the hitter returns the drop shot, the feeder takes another ball and immediately sends another offensive lob over the hitter's head and the cycle is continued.

FOOTWORK IN TENNIS

By

Al Robinson
Plant City, Florida, High School

In our years as a tennis coach, we have found that footwork and timing are two big stumbling blocks for many average players who are capable of becoming outstanding players.

Footwork may appear to be an elementary phase of good tennis, but it is a very basic and important one. We do not think enough time and effort are devoted to this phase of the game. Regardless of how poorly or well a player may play, his success is dependent almost entirely on how well his feet perform. Good footwork on the part of a tennis player entails many factors which must be studied, learned, and practiced well before his game will show genuine improvement. Many players take their footwork for granted, and believe it is a skill that will come to them naturally.

While he is learning the various grips and strokes, the beginning player usually becomes too involved in mastering these rudiments of the sport. Footwork is taught in a very elementary manner which is natural while a boy is learning the game. When a player has learned the basic grips and strokes, he should be more concerned about placing his feet and body in their proper relation to the ball. After a certain stage, stroking the ball will not improve footwork as might be expected, but just the opposite is true. Continued improvement of strokes and timing is possible only through concentration on footwork and body position in relation to the ball.

In most cases, tennis players are unconsciously lazy or do not realize the contribution that good footwork and hustle will make toward improving their game. We have seen boys who could stroke the ball well if it were hit to them just right. Again, we have observed these same players standing flat-footed when the ball landed too close to them, and have noticed that often when running for a ball, they will over-run it. Through overrunning they hit with a bent cramped elbow, and a wild or unpredictable shot is the result. Should such a shot go into his opponent's court, the chances are that the opponent will be able to put the ball away. Tennis players make these mistakes because they do not keep their body weight under control through the proper distribution of weight on and over the balls of their feet.

Many players make the mistake of letting the ball play them, so to speak, instead of mastering the ball and playing it as they should or wish. Proper footwork will allow the player not only to make the type of shot he desires, but also to place the ball where he wishes. In going to the ball or making the stroke, he must keep his body weight under control and slightly forward over the balls of his feet. When the player lets his body weight remain over his heels and has to move to the ball quickly, the first thing he must do is shift the weight of his body over the balls of his feet before he can move. In most instances, he is unable to move quickly enough. How does a player have a chance of getting to a ball that is hit to the corners swiftly, or at a relatively sharp angle if he is standing back in the middle of the baseline or at the net position with his body weight over his heels? The odds are one out of ten, if not greater, that he will not be able to get to the ball in time, or resume the proper position to make a good return.

We have observed players and coached others who would, after they had been able to get over to the side for a corner or angle shot, stand still and wait to see how good their return would be. By the time they managed to get their body weight off their heels and their feet in motion to get back to the center of the court, they were vulnerable either for a shot back to the side they were leaving, a shot to the side which they were farthest from, a short slice or a drop shot. When a player is able to get to the side for the return of a corner or angle shot, he should not wait to see if his shot will be good, whether his opponent will make a good return, or where it will be returned. The proper thing for him to do is to make his shot and then hustle back to the proper position which will give him good general court coverage. This principle applies whether he feels his return will be an ace or an error. He must wait until the point is over before he begins to consider any relaxation.

In each stroke process, the eyes carry a message to the brain. In turn the brain passes the message to the feet, tells them how quickly they must move, and in what direction to go. The player must condition his body and reflexes through practice and concentration so they are ready to respond quickly. A second lost can result in the loss of a point.

Strong concentration on the ball will help the player with his footwork. He must watch the ball closely and also the body position of his opponent as he hits the ball. The body position of the opponent as he strokes the ball can, in many instances, give the player a tip on where it will be hit. Then the player immediately picks up the flight of the ball when his opponent hits it, and eases into position where the ball will land or where he wishes to volley it. This alertness will prevent unnecessary rushing around the court. Good concentration and focus on the ball implies that as it comes closer to the player it will definitely increase in size. If he is concentrating properly when he looks at the ball, it will be clear and the background will be blurred. Poor concentration will cause the background of the ball to be clear and the ball blurred.

A tennis player must learn to take the shortest path to the ball in order to improve his position in relation to it. In most instances, the player will try to take the same path for a majority of the balls hit to him. Each ball hit to the player must be attacked in its own special way to develop the best possible shot and stroke. The path to be taken to each shot will be determined by its depth, height, and the angle at which the ball is hit. If a ball is high and deep enough to volley in the air, the player must move in with his feet and hit it in the proper manner. If a ball is hit at an angle, the player must take an angled path to it and not a parallel path to the baseline or net. Taking a path parallel to the net will result in a hurried and poor shot which gives the opponent time to ready himself for the return, or take the net and have it under his command for a volley return (Diagrams 1 and 2).

After each stroke, a player must keep his feet moving at a slow pace instead of stopping completely and starting. If his feet are stopping and starting, his mind will lag and he loses precious seconds in getting to the ball. Even a second lost at the wrong time can be disastrous. In moving about the court, short steps are preferred over long, awkward ones. With a slight movement of the feet while waiting for the return shot, tension is caused in the muscles which make it possible for the player to move his feet quickly in the direction of the ball.

The player must approach the ball from behind and come up alongside it with the flow of his body weight into the stroke. If he steps with his feet in the proper manner and pulls back with the weight of his body in his stroke, he will execute a poor stroke with just his arm and there will be no body flow

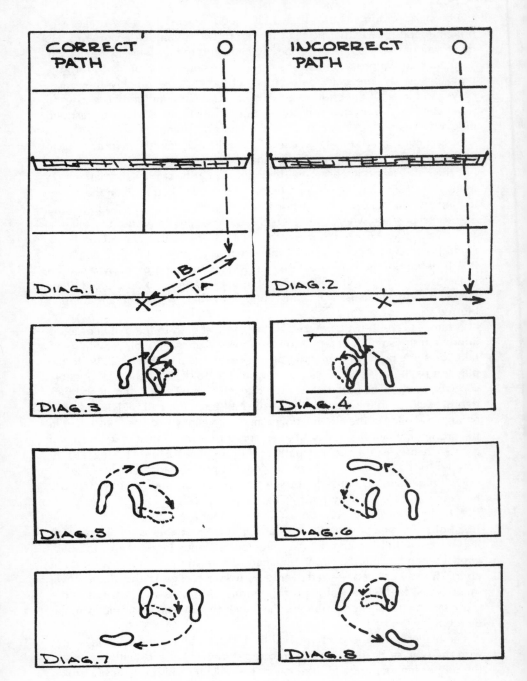

or power in it. In this type of stroke, his muscles are working against each other. In all proper strokes and shots, the player's feet must be in proper relationship to the ball in order to make a proper body flow possible.

Some tips on footwork at the net are as follows:

1) Take a slight hop just before the opponent strokes the ball. This movement will cause tension in the muscles that will make the advance to the ball easier and quicker.

2) Always take a jab step to the ball when it is possible in the volley stroke. Lead with the left foot on the forehand volley and the right foot on the backhand volley (Diagrams 3 and 4).

3) On the forehand volley stroke the player should drop his right foot back and lead with his left foot. On the backhand volley stroke he should drop his right foot (Diagrams 7 and 8).

Some tips on footwork at the baseline are as follows:

1) In stroking, always lead with the front foot. On the forehand stroke a player should lead with his left foot and on a backhand stroke with his right foot (Diagrams 5 and 6).

2) If balls are landing too close to the player, he should drop his right foot back on the forehand stroke and lead with his left foot. On a backhand stroke he should drop his left foot back and lead with his right foot (Diagrams 7 and 8).

3) The first step in going for a ball will depend on how far the player has to go. It can be made with an open or cross step. This is a technique that must be developed to suit the individual (Diagrams 9 and 10).

Exercises are important in helping a player develop better footwork. Some very effective exercises are: Jumping rope, one-legged knee bends, short wind springs of 20 to 30 yards, agility drills, running short distances backwards, road work, and studying and practicing the techniques set forth in this article.

The person who hopes to become a top tennis player should go on the court prepared to give his all and do his best. If he does not have this attitude, he should stay off the court, or at least realize that he cannot expect to be successful except through luck.

ANTICIPATION AND THE INTERMEDIATE TENNIS PLAYER

By

Brian Chamberlain and Dr. Jim Brown
McNeese State University

The intermediate tennis player is often faced with a frustrating problem. He has developed his strokes so that he appears to be as good as advanced players; he has started to develop his own game plans rather than being forced into a style of play by his opponents; however, he loses frequently to players of seemingly equal talent because he does not yet know how to anticipate what is about to happen during a point. His opponents know what he is going to do before he does it, and when he thinks he has the advantage in a particular situation, he loses points because he has been out-anticipated.

A great deal of what players refer to as anticipation is learned through years of experience. If a player learns the game before he is 15 years old and continues to play regularly, by the time he reaches the junior veteran classification, he has had 20 years of seeing shots and being in every conceivable court situation. It is for this reason that older doubles teams can defeat younger players even though the youngsters have the physical edge.

However, the intermediate player, whether in high school, college or out of school, can do three things to make up for the anticipation generation gap. He can know basic tennis strategy, he can familiarize himself with his opponent's playing habits, and he can watch for tipoff signs.

If a player knows basic tennis strategy (and it is assumed that the intermediate player does), he answers the question, *What should my opponent do in a given situation?* What do the principles of sound tennis dictate in this situation? Here are a few of the many examples of percentage shots in tennis: 1. Volleys hit following the serve will be placed deep and cross-court. 2. Approach shots will usually be hit down the line. 3. First serves will usually be placed to the outside in order to pull the receiver off the court. 4. Second serves will be hit with less velocity, but more spin. 5. Offensive lobs will usually be placed to the opponent's backhand side.

If a player is familiar with his opponent's playing habits, he can answer the question, *What does my opponent usually do in this situation?* Almost all players have a favorite side or a favorite shot. Intelligent players will scout their opposition and make mental notes about individual idiosyncrasies, strengths, and weaknesses. If the match is against an unfamiliar opponent, the intermediate player can usually talk to someone who has played against him. Some coaches require their players to make written reports following each match.

After all the strategy is learned, and after the intermediate player has gathered all the information possible about an opponent, he is still faced with the most important question: *What is my opponent going to do this time (on this shot)?* It is in this area that certain suggestions may be valuable. These suggestions will not replace 20 years of experience, but they may cut the gap down enough to make a significant difference in winning or losing a match.

Suggestion No. 1: Watch the opponent's eyes prior to the serve. Many players, even those in the advanced group, inadvertently look at the spot where they plan to serve immediately before the toss. If an opponent is watching him closely enough, he can detect this tip-off sign and adjust accordingly. It may mean moving a step or two to the right, or left, changing from one trip to another, or doing nothing, but having more confidence and purpose in the service return. Whatever it does for a player, it gives him an advantage in games he is expected to lose—the opponent's serve.

Suggestion No. 2: Watch the opponent's feet as he prepares to hit a ground stroke. A closed stance (one in which the feet are approximately parallel to the alley) usually indicates that the next shot is more likely to go down the line than anywhere else. An open stance (one in which the foot closest to the net does not come all the way around) might be a tip-off that a cross-court shot is coming. On the serve if the opponent's feet are almost parallel to the baseline, expect a flat, hard serve. If the feet are staggered, watch for the twist.

Suggestion No. 3: Watch the opponent's racket head as he takes a backswing. If the racket head starts low or moves in a vertical motion rather than a motion horizontal to the court, watch for the topspin shot. When a shot is hit with topspin, the sound will be the same and the motion just as rapid, but the shot will have less velocity than usual, will rise fast, drop fast, and then take an unusually high bounce. If the racket head is drawn straight back, the return is likely to be flat, with good pace, and low to the net. If the racket head goes back high, watch for the chop (underspin). The chop will float a little, bounce lower than other shots, and slow down or bite when it bounces.

Suggestion No. 4: Watch the ball—even when it is on the other side of the net. All tennis players have been taught to keep their eyes on the ball as they hit. Few players have been taught to watch the ball as the other player prepares to hit. For example, when a right handed player serving from the right side tosses the ball up on the right side of his body, he is likely to serve closer to the middle of the court. If he tosses the ball across his body to the left, watch for the serve to go to the outside of the service court.

Watch how the ball bounces prior to the opponent's ground strokes. The ball may slide as it bounces, causing him to hit up. It may hit a line, crack or object on the court, throwing his timing off. The ball may bounce closer to him than he expected, usually causing him to hit up without an angle, and with little pace.

Suggestion No. 5: Be aware of the court position of the opponent. He or she can do only certain things in certain situations. As an example, a player is at the net, and hits a short volley. His opponent is well back in the court and has to charge forward and stretch to reach the ball. In this situation it is practically impossible for him to pick the ball up enough to clear a man who is standing at the net. The player who is volleying can move in even closer to the net and expect the shot to come at him head high.

Another example is when the player is at the net the opponent lobs over his head. As he goes back to play the lob off the bounce, he should sneak a glance at the opponent. Is he standing still? Is he charging the net or just loafing in? Running back and looking over the shoulder instead of at the ball may be the epitome of optimism, but it is worth the effort if it wins one point per match.

ANTICIPATION requires as much or more concentration as hitting the ball.

A third example is when the opponent is at the net, and the player attempts a lob to his backhand side. If the lob is high enough to make him stretch, but not high enough to clear him, the chances are good that he will go cross-court with his volley. Although there are exceptions to this probability, the player can take a chance and make an early move in the proper direction, hopefully making a winner out of the next shot.

Careful observation of these tip-off signs, combined with knowledge of basic strategy and an opponent's habits, will enable the intermediate player to have a reasonably accurate guess about what is going to happen in many situations. Anticipation requires as much or more concentration as hitting the ball. Decisions based on partial evidence must be made in fractions of seconds. But partial evidence is better than no evidence at all, and by anticipating a shot, a player can begin to move into position and get his racket ready a few seconds sooner. These few seconds are precious, and become increasingly more precious as a player improves and meets a higher caliber of competition.

THE KEY TO WINNING TENNIS IS RACKET PREPARATION

By

Larry Castle
Middle Tennessee State University

and

Powell D. McClellan
Middle Tennessee State University

High school and college coaches are always looking for new drills and methods to improve the play of their tennis players. Most coaches, as well as players, are aware of the importance of fundamentals, and numerous hours are spent practicing footwork, keeping the eye on the ball, charging the net, and keeping a firm wrist at contact. However, the player may perform all of the previously mentioned fundamentals properly and still make a poor shot due to improper preparation of the racket.

We place considerable emphasis upon the proper position of the racket prior, during, and after each stroke. During the last several years many of our players performed outstandingly in one match and then poorly in the next. After careful observation we concluded that one possible reason for this inconsistency was poor racket preparation. Therefore, in order to assist our players in analyzing their racket preparation, the following guide was developed.

In the ready position (Illustration 1), the racket is held firmly in the left hand with the throat resting on the fingers of the right hand. In this position the head of the racket should not be dropped, and the racket should be held firmly in one hand.

Coaching Point: Check the position of the racket head each time the ready position is assumed. Make sure that the head of the racket is pointed slightly up and over the right net post.

Once the player sees the ball coming to his forehand, he pivots on his back foot (Illustration 2) and the racket is drawn back by using the left hand. Notice that the racket is slightly above the waist, and the player's right hand is still on the throat of the racket.

205

Illustration #1

Illustration #2

Illustration #3

Illustration #4

Illustration #5

Illustration #6

> Coaching Point: Keeping the right hand on the throat of the racket will assure that the player keeps his right shoulder low and into the net.

As the ball approaches the player (Illustration 3), the right hand releases the racket and the left arm extends backward.

> Coaching Point: After the right hand releases the racket, the player should continue to extend his left arm until the racket points to the fence behind the player.

One common fault we have noticed is that the novice player will often develop a waggle of the racket at this stage of his stroke. This waggle may be attributed to either the right hand pushing rather than releasing the racket, or the left wrist and arm not being completely extended. To correct a waggle of the racket, we emphasize a firm wrist and fully extended elbow.

Illustration 4 shows the player starting his forward swing immediately before contact is made with the ball. Notice that the racket head is held steady and will come through slightly behind the player's wrist and elbow.

> Coaching Point: Emphasize to the players that the racket should feel as though it is being pulled through rather than pushed through.

A common mistake often made by beginning tennis players is to lead with the elbow which causes the head of the racket to come through first. The player should sense a pulling sensation of the elbow rather than a feeling of pushing. We attempt to teach the kinesthetic sense of this type of movement by continuous practice until it becomes automatic.

After the ball has been hit, the player should begin preparation for the next stroke (Illustration 5). He should analyze mentally the placement of his stroke and begin to anticipate where his opponent will return the shot.

> Coaching Point: At this stage the player should begin mental preparation for the next shot.

Finally, the player completes his stroke with a high follow-through (Illustration 6). The high follow-through is emphasized so that the ball will remain in contact with the surface of the racket as long as possible which enables the player to control his shot more readily. After the follow-through, once again the player returns to the ready position.

It is the feeling of most tennis coaches that through constant practice and repetition most players will develop the proper fundamentals of tennis. We sincerely believe that the same principle applies to racket preparation. Only through constant practice and correct coaching techniques can proper racket preparation be accomplished.

CHAMPIONSHIP
TENNIS
by the experts